Understanding the
BIOCHEMISTRY
OF RESPIRATION

D. C. James, BSc., P.G.C.E.
Biology Teacher   Seaford Head School
East Sussex

G. S. Matthews, BSc., P.G.C.E.
Head of Biology   Seaford Head School
East Sussex

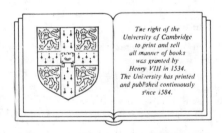

The right of the
University of Cambridge
to print and sell
all manner of books
was granted by
Henry VIII in 1534.
The University has printed
and published continuously
since 1584.

CAMBRIDGE UNIVERSITY PRESS

Cambridge
London   New York   Port Chester
Melbourne   Sydney

Published by the Press Syndicate of the University of Cambridge
The Pitt Building, Trumpington Street, Cambridge CB2 1RP
40 West 20th Street, New York, NY 10011, USA
10 Stamford Road, Oakleigh, Melbourne 3166, Australia

© Cambridge University Press 1991

First published 1991

Printed in Great Britain by Scotprint Ltd

British Library cataloguing-in-publication data
Matthews, G. S.
    Understanding the biochemistry of respiration.
    1. Organisms. Respiration
    I. Title II. James, D. C. (David C)
    574.12

ISBN 0–521–39993–9

NOTICE TO TEACHERS

Acknowledgements

Many people have played a part in shaping the final format of this book. In particular we would like to thank Alan Miller, Head of Science, Seaford Head School and David Hutton, Second in Science, St Paul's School, Haywards Heath, for their careful checking of the chemical details involved in the first chapter. Thanks are also due to our sixth form students Carl Stevenson and Sam Hodgson for their enthusiasm in reading the completed manuscript and giving us a view of the book through students' eyes. All their comments were greatly appreciated, if not always acted upon. Finally we would like to thank Karen and Kathryn for their support and encouragement throughout the project, particularly Kathryn for undertaking the arduous task of typing the entire manuscript.

Table A2.1 is taken from *Biological Science Volume 1* (1984) N. P. O. Green *et al.*, Cambridge University Press. Figure A5.1 is adapted from *Biology: A Functional Approach* (1986) 4th Edition, M. B. V. Roberts, Nelson, and Figure A7.1 is reproduced from *Enzymes, Energy and Metabolism* (1986) M. R. Ingle, Blackwell.
Figure 2.2 from Focal Point Audio Visual Ltd/Dr S. Bradbury; Figure 2.4 from Biophoto Associates; Figure 2.6 from Dr Brij L. Gupta, University of Cambridge.

Cover photo: An artist's impression of a mitochondrion surrounding a cell vesicle © Francis Leroy, Biocosmos/Science Photo Library.

Contents

Preface

A popular misconception among sixth-form students is that advanced-level biology is the 'easy option' of the three core sciences. The problem with this is that any detailed treatment of biological systems almost inevitably leads to complex molecular structures and pathways – biochemistry, in short! The concise but detailed accounts found in the standard advanced-level texts often assume a level of understanding and knowledge which in our experience is only possessed by a small percentage of very able students.

The aim of this book is to guide you through the variety of complex biochemical pathways which make up cellular respiration in a clear, step-by-step, easy-to-follow format. Whilst endeavouring to keep the material accessible we have found it necessary in places to probe beyond the depth required by many of the advanced-level syllabuses. We considered this essential in order to fully explain certain concepts, and also to provide the additional information often demanded by more able students. Consequently this book will also prove a valuable resource to first-year undergraduates in the biological sciences.

We have arranged the text in eight chapters, each divided into clearly labelled sections for ease of reference. To develop a more complete understanding the major biochemical pathways have been broken up into a series of numbered stages, each of which is then discussed in detail.

The text also includes questions of the type commonly raised by our A-level students. These are boxed in the text. Although answers are provided we hope the questions will make you pause for thought and so consider the topic in greater depth. For revision purposes, the essential facts in chapters 3–8 have been summarised at the end of each chapter in the form of easily memorised diagrams and numbered points.

Chapter 1, Basic biochemistry, is included for non-chemists and for those who feel their biochemistry would benefit from a little basic revision. Finally, the appendices provide useful additional information, much of which the larger texts again assume to be prior knowledge.

We have written this book with the intention that it will be read chapter by chapter to enable the progressive development of a more complete understanding of cellular respiration. But whichever way you choose to read it, we hope it will provide an interesting and stimulating voyage through some of the intricacies of cell metabolism.

1 Basic biochemistry

This chapter contains only that biochemical knowledge that has direct revelance to the understanding of cellular respiration – it is not intended as a comprehensive guide to biochemistry. The information is arranged under the following headings:

(a)   Atomic structure
(b)   Bonding
(c)   Oxidation and reduction
(d)   Decarboxylation
(e)   Dissociation
(f)   Adenosine triphosphate (ATP)
(g)   Enzymes
(h)   Nicotinamide adenine dinucleotide (NAD).

(a) Atomic structure

An **atom** is the smallest part of an element that can exist independently. Atoms contain three types of particle: **protons**, **neutrons** and **electrons**. Table 1.1 gives data about these particles.

Table 1.1 *Atomic particle data*

Particle	Charge	Mass	Position in atom
Proton	+1	1 unit*	Cluster together to form the central nucleus of the atom
Neutron	0	1 unit*	
Electron	−1	$\frac{1}{1870}$ unit*	Orbit the nucleus

*1 unit $= 1.7 \times 10^{-24}$ g

Atoms are electrically neutral since the number of positively charged protons in the nucleus is the same as the number of negatively charged electrons orbiting it.

The **atomic number** is the number of protons making up the nucleus of an atom. It also equals the number of electrons in the atom.

The **mass number** or **atomic mass** is the total mass of the protons and neutrons making up the nucleus of the atom. (The mass of an electron is so small it is ignored.)

For example, oxygen's atomic number is 8 and its mass number is 16.

This may be written as: $^{16}_{8}\text{O}$

Thus the oxygen atom has 8 protons, and therefore 8 electrons. It also has 8 neutrons, giving it a mass number of 16.

Isotopes

The atoms of certain elements exist in different forms. Each form has the same number of protons and electrons (otherwise it would be a different element) but different numbers of neutrons. So different forms of the element have the same atomic number but different mass numbers.

For example, naturally occurring chlorine consists of 75% of the ^{35}Cl isotope and 25% of the ^{37}Cl isotope.

The **relative atomic mass (RAM)** of an element is the average of the mass numbers of the isotopes of the element. The proportions of the naturally occurring isotopes of chlorine are such that its RAM is 35.5.

Electron arrangement

The electrons orbit the nucleus in a series of shells around it. There may be up to seven of these shells, at different energy levels. Each shell can hold a fixed maximum number of electrons. The electrons in the shells closest to the nucleus have the least energy while those furthest away have the most.

The addition of extra energy, for example light energy, may enable an electron to 'jump' to a higher energy level. The electron will invariably return to its original energy level, releasing the extra energy as it does so as heat and light (fluorescence). If these **excited** electrons can be 'captured' before returning to their original energy level the extra energy they possess may be used to drive certain biological processes. For example, photosynthesis uses electron acceptors to capture light-excited electrons; their energy is then used to drive the synthesis of complex organic molecules.

The maximum number of electrons that can be held in each of the first four shells is shown below.

First shell (K shell):   **2 electrons**
Second shell (L shell):   **8 electrons**
Third shell (M shell)*:   **18 electrons**
Fourth shell (N shell)*:   **32 electrons**

*The third and fourth shells do not fill evenly. As a result, the fourth shell begins to fill up when the third shell has only eight electrons in it.

Table 1.2 gives atomic data for the first 20 elements, including their electron arrangements.

Table 1.2 *Atomic data for the first 20 elements*

Element	Symbol	Atomic number	Mass number	RAM	Electron arrangement K	L	M	N
Hydrogen	H	1	1	1.0	1			
Helium	He	2	4	4.0	2			
Lithium	Li	3	7	6.9	2	1		
Beryllium	Be	4	9	9.0	2	2		
Boron	B	5	11	10.8	2	3		
Carbon	C	6	12	12.0	2	4		
Nitrogen	N	7	14	14.0	2	5		
Oxygen	O	8	16	16.0	2	6		
Fluorine	F	9	19	19.0	2	7		
Neon	Ne	10	20	20.2	2	8		
Sodium	Na	11	23	23.0	2	8	1	
Magnesium	Mg	12	24	24.3	2	8	2	
Aluminium	Al	13	27	27.0	2	8	3	
Silicon	Si	14	28	28.1	2	8	4	
Phosphorus	P	15	31	31.0	2	8	5	
Sulphur	S	16	32	32.1	2	8	6	
Chlorine	Cl	17	35	35.5	2	8	7	
Argon	Ar	18	40	39.9	2	8	8	
Potassium	K	19	39	39.1	2	8	8	1
Calcium	Ca	20	40	40.1	2	8	8	2

An atom of an element which has a full outermost shell is particularly stable and therefore unreactive, e.g. both helium (2) and neon (2,8) have atoms with full outer shells and seldom react with other elements. Because of the stability conferred by full outer shells, all elements 'strive' to obtain full outer electron shells when reacting with other elements to form compounds. During these reactions, **ionic** or **covalent bonds** may be formed.

(b) Bonding

(i) Ionic bonding

In **ionic bonding** electrons are lost or gained from an atom in order to attain a full outer electron shell. When an atom loses or gains an electron it becomes a charged particle or **ion**. The loss of one electron leaves the atom with a net charge of $+1$ (since the nucleus still has the same number of protons). Similarly the gaining of one electron leaves the atom with a net charge of -1.

Figure 1.1 shows the electron arrangements of sodium and chlorine. (Different symbols are used for electrons in each atom, but all electrons are in fact identical.) Clearly sodium needs to lose one electron from its outer shell whilst chlorine needs to gain an electron in its outer shell if both atoms are to achieve full outer shells. Figure 1.2 shows the electron arrangements of sodium and chloride ions.

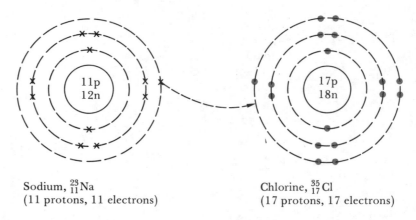

Sodium, $^{23}_{11}$Na
(11 protons, 11 electrons)

Chlorine, $^{35}_{17}$Cl
(17 protons, 17 electrons)

Figure 1.1   *Electron arrangements of sodium and chlorine*

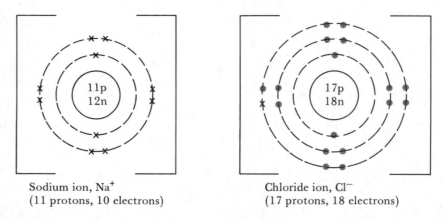

Sodium ion, Na$^+$
(11 protons, 10 electrons)

Chloride ion, Cl$^-$
(17 protons, 18 electrons)

Figure 1.2   *Electron arrangements of sodium and chloride ions in the compound sodium chloride*

The two oppositely charged ions attract one another, forming an **ionic bond**. The resulting **ionic compound** consists of ions with full outer shells and is therefore stable.

(ii) Covalent bonding

In the formation of **covalent bonds** electrons are not lost or gained; instead they are shared. For example, chlorine atoms have seven electrons in their outer shells, so they need to gain one electron in order to achieve a full outer shell. This is accomplished by two chlorine atoms sharing a pair of electrons, as shown in Figure 1.3.

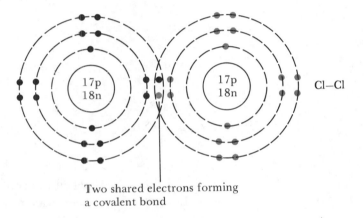

Two shared electrons forming
a covalent bond

Figure 1.3   *Electron arrangement of the chlorine molecule*

The bonded atoms form a **molecule** of chlorine (Cl_2). The two atoms sharing the pair of electrons are held together by a covalent bond. This is written conventionally as Cl—Cl. Oxygen atoms form molecules (O_2) by sharing two pairs of electrons, and therefore form double bonds, i.e. O=O.

Atoms of different elements can also share electrons, forming **covalent compounds**, as shown in Figure 1.4.

(c) Oxidation and reduction

(i) Oxidation

Substances may be **oxidised** in one of three ways:

1.   Direct addition of oxygen – this is rare in biological systems.

2.   Removal of hydrogen atoms (H). This is also called **dehydrogenation**. It is by far the most common means of oxidation in biological

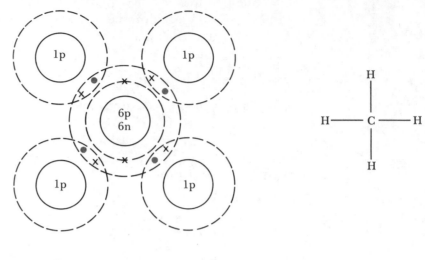

Carbon $^{12}_{6}C$

Hydrogen $^{1}_{1}H$

Figure 1.4 *In methane carbon gains a share of four electrons, while each hydrogen gains a share of one*

systems. Within cells, special molecules called **coenzymes** usually accept the hydrogen atoms, becoming reduced in the process, for example:

$$\textbf{NAD} \quad + \quad \textbf{2H} \quad \longrightarrow \quad \textbf{NADH}_2$$

coenzyme   hydrogen   reduced
               atoms   coenzyme

3. Removal of electrons. A hydrogen atom can be considered to be a proton (H^+) and an electron (e^-). In fact hydrogen carriers like NAD (see page 13) carry the hydrogens as protons and electrons. Consequently removal of hydrogen atoms and removal of electrons usually occur simultaneously. However, under certain circumstances only electrons may be removed, for example the passage of electrons through the cytochrome carriers of the ETC (electron transfer chain – see chapter 5).

(ii) Reduction

Similarly, substances may be **reduced** in three ways:

1. Removal of oxygen – again rare in biological systems.

2. Addition of hydrogen atoms. In biological systems the hydrogen atoms required for reduction are usually supplied by reduced

coenzymes (like $NADH_2$). By donating its hydrogen atoms the coenzyme is itself oxidised in the process, for example:

$$NADH_2 + X \longrightarrow XH_2 + NAD$$

| reduced coenzyme | substrate | reduced substrate | oxidised coenzyme |

3. Addition of electrons, for example the passage of electrons through the ETC as described above. Clearly oxidation and reduction always occur together since the oxidation of one substance brings about the reduction of the second substance, for example:

$$NADH_2 + X \longrightarrow XH_2 + NAD$$

In order to reduce substance X the reduced coenzyme ($NADH_2$) is itself oxidised. Such reactions are termed **redox** reactions (see chapter 5).

(d) *Decarboxylation*

Quite simply, **decarboxylation** is the removal of carbon dioxide. These reactions are catalysed by enzymes called *decarboxylases* (see chapter 4), for example the oxidative decarboxylation of pyruvic acid to form acetyl coenzyme A (acetyl CoA):

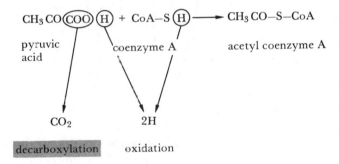

(e) *Dissociation*

In any aqueous solution a very small proportion of water molecules split spontaneously into protons (H^+) and hydroxide ions (OH^-); a process termed **dissociation**:

$$H_2O \longrightarrow H^+ + OH^-$$

| water molecule | proton | hydroxide ion |

Therefore the cytoplasm of a cell contains protons and hydroxide ions in solution. This supply of free protons is particularly important in

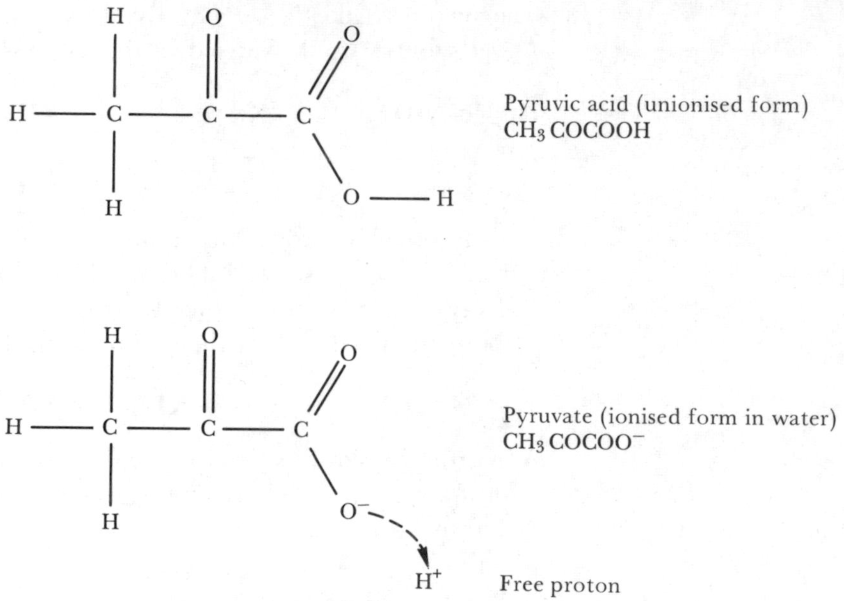

Pyruvic acid (unionised form)
$CH_3 COCOOH$

Pyruvate (ionised form in water)
$CH_3 COCOO^-$

Free proton

Figure 1.5   *Pyruvic acid and pyruvate*

hydrogen carriage (see NAD/FAD, page 13) and the synthesis of ATP (see chapter 6).

Many substances release protons when they dissociate – such substances are called **acids**. Many of the respiratory intermediates, particularly those of the Krebs cycle (see chapter 4), behave in this way and act as proton donors. Compounds like this can therefore exist in two forms, as shown for pyruvic acid in Figure 1.5.

Both names refer to the same compound. Different texts tend to use one or other or even both terms – obviously this can be somewhat confusing. Throughout this book we shall use only the '-ic acid' terminology since it helps to clarify the understanding of certain reactions, for example the oxidative decarboxylation of pyruvic acid discussed above.

It should be noted, however, that in any solution both forms will exist in equilibrium, for example:

$$CH_3 COCOOH \rightleftharpoons CH_3 COCOO^- + H^+$$

pyruvic acid   pyruvate

The relative quantities of each depend on the **pH** (proton concentration, $[H^+]$) of the solution in which the pyruvic acid is dissolved. In the cytoplasm the majority of pyruvic acid molecules are present in the unionised form since pyruvic acid is a weak acid.

(f) *Adenosine triphosphate (ATP)*

The primary function of respiration is the generation of free energy. Much of this energy is stored within the high-energy phosphoanhydride bonds of **adenosine triphosphate** molecules (**ATP**).

ATP is a nucleotide made up of the nitrogenous base **adenine** (a purine base containing two rings), the pentose (five-carbon) sugar **ribose** and a string of three **phosphate** groups ($-PO_3^{2-}$), as shown in Figure 1.6.

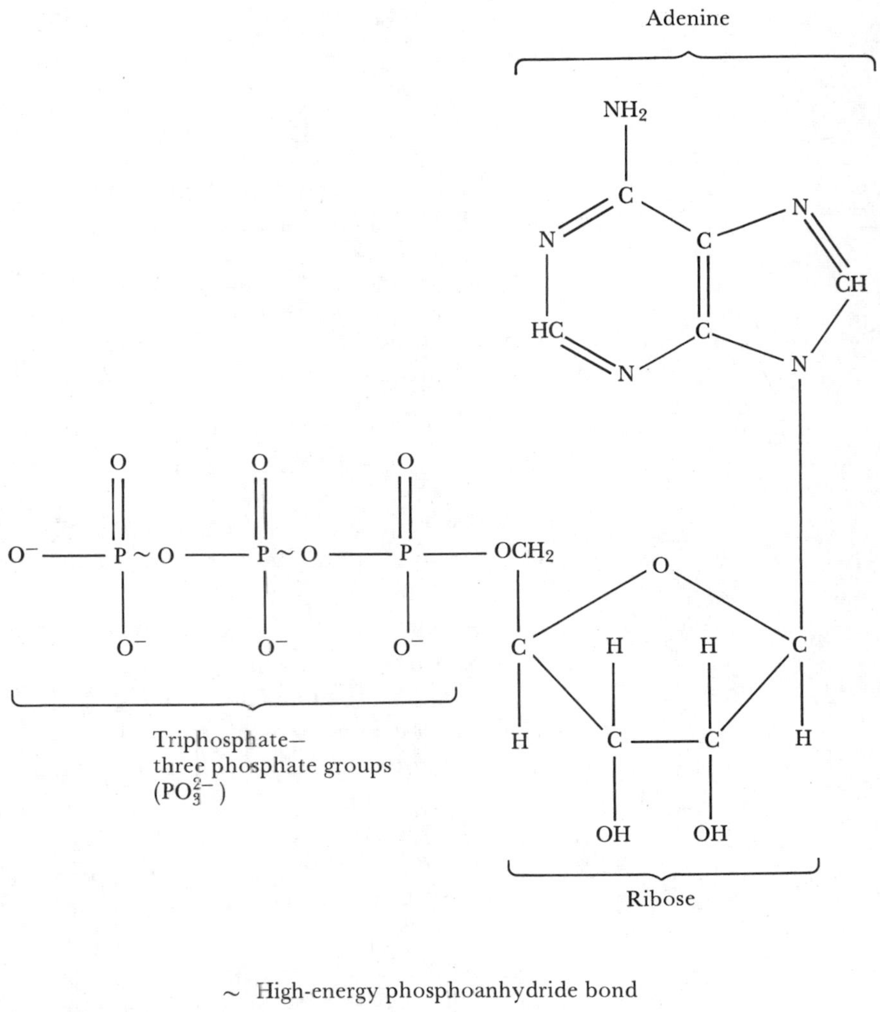

~ High-energy phosphoanhydride bond

Figure 1.6   *The structure of ATP*

Adenine + ribose = adenosine; hence the name adenosine triphosphate. It can be represented more simply as

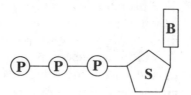

This molecule is derived from **adenosine monophosphate** (**AMP**):

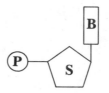

The addition of a single phosphate group produces **adenosine diphosphate** (**ADP**) – their reaction requires 30.6 kJ of energy per mole:

AMP + P + 30.6 kJ ⟶ ADP

Similarly, the addition of a second phosphate group produces adenosine triphosphate (ATP) and also requires 30.6 kJ of energy per mole:

ADP + P + 30.6 kJ ⟶ ATP

The energy required for these **phosphorylation** (addition of phosphate) reactions is the energy released during the oxidation of foodstuffs.

Since energy cannot be created or destroyed (the first law of thermodynamics) it remains 'trapped' within the phosphoanhydride bonds of the ATP molecule. Subsequent hydrolysis of these bonds releases this energy which can be used to drive a variety of biochemical processes including muscle contraction, active transport and biosynthesis.

In practice only the first hydrolysis, to ADP, is carried out. Rarely is ATP fully hydrolysed to AMP. It is quicker for the cell to regenerate ATP from ADP than from AMP so it is more efficient to hydrolyse only to ADP.

Since ATP serves as the principal donor of free energy in biological systems it is generated and consumed extremely quickly. Typically a molecule of ATP is used within a minute of its production. A resting person may use up to 2 kg of ATP per hour.

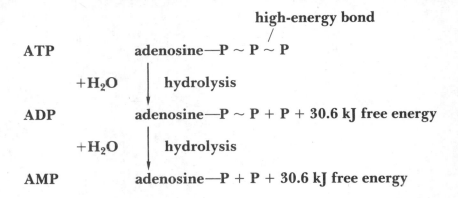

$$\text{ATP} \qquad \text{adenosine—P} \sim \text{P} \sim \text{P}$$

high-energy bond

$+H_2O$ | hydrolysis

$$\text{ADP} \qquad \text{adenosine—P} \sim \text{P} + \text{P} + 30.6 \text{ kJ free energy}$$

$+H_2O$ | hydrolysis

$$\text{AMP} \qquad \text{adenosine—P} + \text{P} + 30.6 \text{ kJ free energy}$$

(g) *Enzymes*

The complex biochemical reactions that comprise cellular respiration are each controlled by a specific **enzyme** or group of enzymes. Enzymes are globular proteins which catalyse reactions by lowering the **activation energy** (the energy required to initiate reactions). This is achieved by providing a surface on which molecules can come close enough to react. Without enzymes such reactions would only occur as a result of random collisions and would not proceed at a rate sufficient to sustain life. The molecules which react on an enzyme surface are called its **substrates**.

Enzymes are large molecules consisting of one or more polypeptide chains, coiled and folded to form a globular unit. Each chain may comprise thousands of amino acids, although only a very small proportion of these (up to 15) may interact with the substrate. The region of the protein which does this is termed the **active site**, and generally appears as a groove or crevice in the surface of the enzyme.

The mechanism of enzyme action is thought to be one of **induced fit** – the substrate modifies the active site as it binds to the enzyme, resulting in an exact fit rather like a hand fitting into a glove, as shown in Figure 1.7.

Enzyme-mediated reactions such as this occur extremely quickly, for example the enzyme *catalase* can hydrolyse 40 000 molecules of hydrogen peroxide to water and oxygen every second!

Many enzymes require additional non-protein substances called **cofactors** in order to work efficiently. There are three main types of cofactor:

(i)   **Inorganic ions**
(ii)   **Coenzymes**
(iii) **Prosthetic groups.**

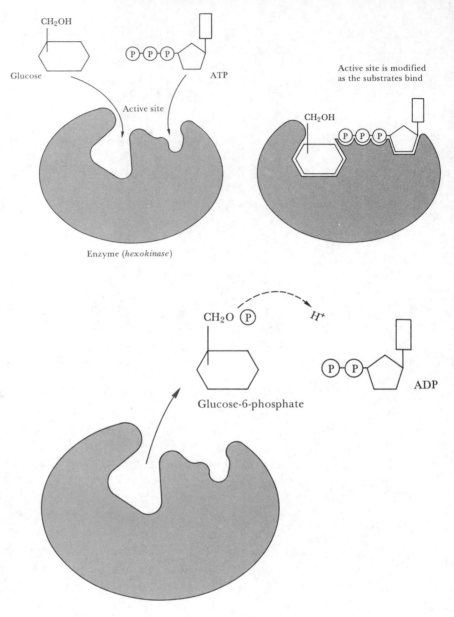

Figure 1.7 *A diagrammatic representation of the phosphorylation of glucose by hexokinase (see chapter 3)*

For example, catalase requires the presence of iron ions to bind effectively with its substrate, hydrogen peroxide. Coenzymes and prosthetic groups are organic molecules which also assist in the formation of the enzyme–substrate complex at the active site. Coenzymes are only loosely associated with their enzyme, while prosthetic groups are more closely associated – they can be looked upon as built-in coenzymes.

(h) *Nicotinamide adenine dinucleotide (NAD)*

A coenzyme with particular significance in respiration is **nicotinamide adenine dinucleotide (NAD)**. NAD's role as a coenzyme is to accept hydrogen atoms from the active site of the dehydrogenase enzyme it is associated with. It is the most important hydrogen carrier in biochemical systems. Its structure is shown in Figure 1.8.

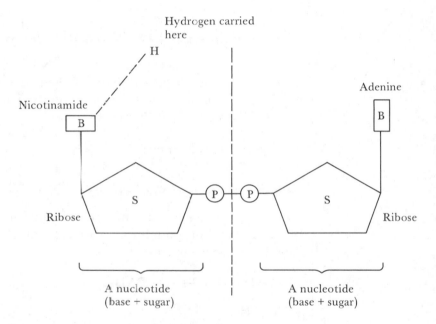

Figure 1.8 *Nicotinamide adenine dinucleotide (NAD)*

The nicotinamide base is the functional hydrogen-carrying part of the molecule. The pairs of hydrogen atoms removed by dehydrogenase enzymes during respiration readily dissociate into protons and electrons:

$$2H \rightleftharpoons 2H^+ + 2e^-$$

The NAD molecule is electron deficient (NAD^+) and so it carries hydrogen atoms as separate protons and electrons. Each molecule of NAD carries one proton and two electrons (in effect, a hydride ion). It accepts the second electron because it is already electron deficient (positively charged).

$$\text{NAD}^+ \quad + \quad 2\text{H}^+ + 2\text{e}^- \quad \longrightarrow \quad \text{NADH} \quad + \quad \text{H}^+$$

oxidised   two hydrogen atoms   reduced   free proton
form   form

When NADH is subsequently reoxidised it gives up a hydrogen atom (1 proton + 1 electron) and the extra electron. Since protons are freely available in the cell cytoplasm the extra electron will immediately combine with a proton, reforming a hydrogen atom. The end result is the release of two hydrogen atoms. Consequently NAD's function as a hydrogen carrier can be summarised as:

$$\text{NAD} \quad + \quad 2\text{H} \quad \longrightarrow \quad \text{NADH}_2$$

oxidised   reduced

Nicotinamide adenine dinucleotide phosphate (NADP)

NADP has the same structure as NAD but with an additional phosphate group attached to one of the ribose units. It also serves as a hydrogen carrier providing reducing power within the cell (see pentose phosphate pathway – chapter 8).

$$\text{NADP} + 2\text{H} \longrightarrow \text{NADPH}_2$$

Flavin adenine dinucleotide (FAD)

FAD is a hydrogen-carrying prosthetic group. It has a role similar to NAD but accepts both the hydrogen atoms ($2\text{H}^+ + 2\text{e}^-$) released by its dehydrogenase enzyme:

$$\text{FAD} + 2\text{H} \longrightarrow \text{FADH}_2$$

The role of NAD/FAD in respiration therefore is to remove high-energy electrons from respiratory intermediates in the manner described above. These high-energy electrons are transferred to a chain of electron carrier molecules. As the electrons are transferred from one carrier to the next their energy is used to pump protons across the inner mitochondrial membrane, creating a proton gradient. It is the energy within this gradient which drives the synthesis of ATP (see chapter 5).

2 Introduction to respiration

Respiration

Respiration is the process by which complex organic molecules are broken down to release energy. It is often summarised as follows:

$$C_6H_{12}O_6 + 6O_2 \longrightarrow 6CO_2 + 6H_2O + 2880 \text{ kJ/mol}$$

glucose   oxygen   carbon dioxide   water   energy

This equation is somewhat misleading in that it makes the following assumptions:

(a) Glucose is the sole respiratory substrate.
(b) The process requires the presence of oxygen.
(c) 2880 kJ of energy are released in a single step.

These assumptions are all incorrect. Cellular respiration proceeds via a series of enzyme-controlled stages in which the chemical bond energy of a variety of different food molecules is liberated. The controlled release of small amounts of energy from each reaction enables the energy to be captured within the energy-rich phosphoanhydride bonds of the nucleotide adenosine triphosphate (ATP). In this way much of the energy released can be stored in a usable form. Subsequent hydrolysis of ATP provides the energy required to power mechanical work, biosynthesis and active transport processes.

Respiration is essentially an **aerobic** process, requiring the presence of oxygen in order to completely oxidise food molecules. It will proceed in the absence of oxygen, however, although the food molecules are only partially oxidised. **Anaerobic** respiration therefore produces less energy and results in the accumulation of partially oxidised food molecules (see chapter 7).

For convenience, respiration may be divided into three distinct stages:

(a) **Glycolysis** (Embden–Meyerhof pathway)
(b) **Krebs cycle** (tricarboxylic acid cycle)
(c) **Electron transfer chain** (respiratory chain).

Their interaction is shown in Figure 2.1.

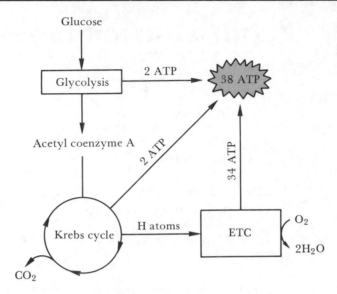

Figure 2.1   *Outline of aerobic respiration and ATP production*

The enzymes controlling the glycolytic pathway are located in the cell cytoplasm. During these reactions a glucose molecule is broken down and eventually split into two molecules of pyruvic acid. These pyruvic acid molecules then enter the matrix of the mitochondrion where the enzymes controlling the Krebs cycle are found. The overall strategy behind this cyclic series of reactions is the removal of pairs of hydrogen atoms from pyruvic acid. These hydrogen pairs are accepted by the hydrogen-carrying coenzyme nicotinamide adenine dinucleotide (NAD) which passes them on to a series of carrier proteins embedded in the inner mitochondrial membrane.

These carriers are collectively termed the electron transfer chain (ETC). Electrons derived from the hydrogen atoms are passed from one carrier to the next, providing the energy required to generate molecules of ATP.

The detailed biochemistry of each of these stages will be discussed in the next three chapters. Their locations in the cell are shown in Figure 2.2.

Mitochondria

Mitochondria are the metabolic 'power stations' of cells, housing the biochemical machinery required to transform the potential energy in glucose molecules into bond energy in ATP. Mitochondria exist in a variety of shapes and generally measure about 1.5–10 μm long by

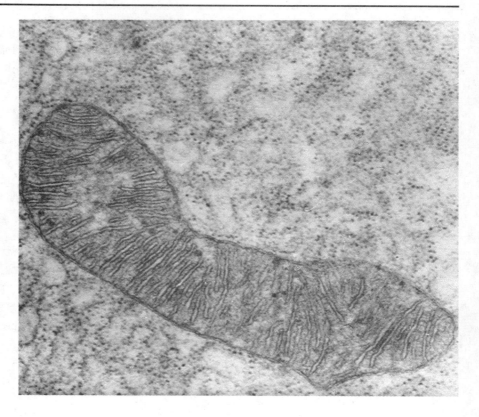

Figure 2.2   *The location of respiratory stages within the cell,* × *50 000*

0.25–1 μm wide. Each mitochondrion is bounded by an envelope of two membranes which enclose a narrow (6–10 nm) fluid-filled space. The surface area of the innermost membrane is greatly increased by the presence of numerous infoldings called **cristae** extending into the central matrix, as shown by Figures 2.3 and 2.4.

The enzymes controlling the Krebs cycle are located within the matrix whilst the carriers of the electron transfer chain are embedded throughout the lipid bilayer of the innermost membrane. The stalked particles responsible for the final synthesis of ATP (see chapter 6) are found encrusting the matrix side of this inner membrane. Figures 2.5 and 2.6 show the detailed structure of the inner membrane.

It should be noted that although the stalked particles generally appear to project into the matrix, this is probably a preparation artefact. In the living cell they are likely to be embedded more deeply in the membrane.

The increase in surface area provided by the cristae allows for greater numbers of electron carriers and stalked particles. This enables the relatively small mitochondrion to produce substantial quantities of

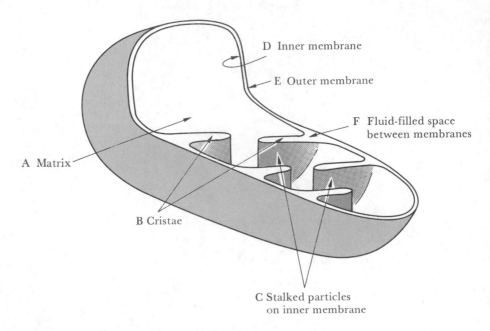

A Matrix

D Inner membrane

E Outer membrane

F Fluid-filled space
between membranes

B Cristae

C Stalked particles
on inner membrane

Figure 2.3   *The structure of a mitochondrion*

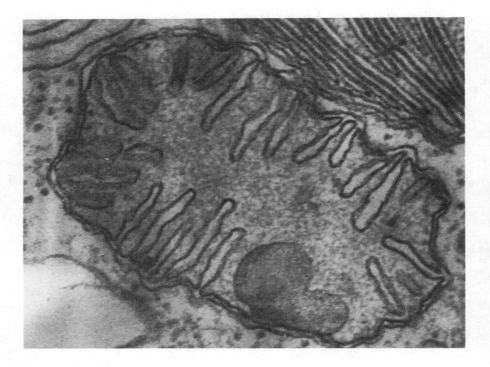

Figure 2.4   *Electron micrograph of a mitochondrion, × 95 000*

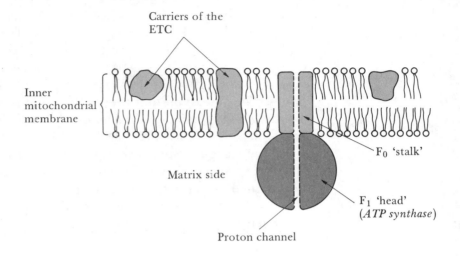

Carriers of the
ETC

Inner
mitochondrial
membrane

F_0 'stalk'

Matrix side

F_1 'head'
(*ATP synthase*)

Proton channel

Figure 2.5   *Organisation of a stalked particle*

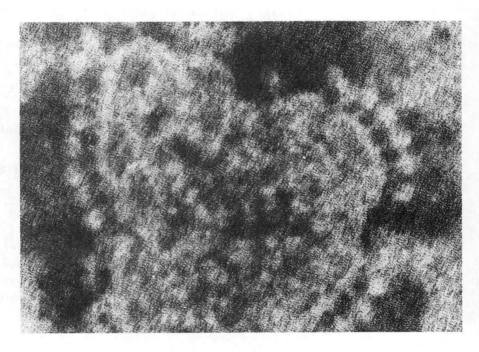

Figure 2.6   *Electron micrograph of a stalked particle, × 600 000*

ATP. Indeed cells with a high energy demand (e.g. liver cells) possess not only large numbers of mitochondria but mitochondria with large numbers of cristae.

It is worth noting at this point that mitochondria possess their own DNA and ribosomes – in other words all the necessary machinery to build their own proteins. However, somewhat unexpectedly, mitochondrial DNA is circular like that of prokaryotic organisms and the ribosomes are the small (70S) type, another feature typical of prokaryotes. The **endosymbiont theory** was proposed in the early 1960s in an attempt to explain these anomalies. It states that both mitochondria and chloroplasts probably evolved from bacteria-like prokaryotes which were engulfed by a primitive eukaryotic organism resulting in a symbiotic association. Over the millions of years that followed many of the original prokaryotic genes were transferred into the eukaryotic nucleus, helping to explain why certain nuclear genes resemble bacterial genes.

The efficiency of respiration

This may be calculated in the following way:

Energy yield for complete oxidation of 1 mole of glucose (from calorimeter studies)	**2880 kJ**
Energy yield for hydrolysis of 1 mole of ATP to ADP	**30.6 kJ**
Total ATP yield/mole of glucose in aerobic respiration	**38 moles of ATP**
Total energy yield/mole of glucose in aerobic respiration	**38 × 30.6 kJ = 1162.8 kJ**
Therefore % efficiency of aerobic respiration	$\dfrac{1162.8}{2880} \times 100\%$ $= 40\%$

This compares well with petrol engines, which only have an efficiency of 25%. The remaining energy is lost as heat and in birds and mammals contributes towards the maintenance of a high body temperature.

3 Glycolysis

Glycolysis

Glycolysis (glycos = sugar, lysis = splitting) is common to **both** aerobic and anaerobic respiration. It does not require oxygen. It is **the** process by which the respiratory substrate (glucose) is first phosphorylated and subsequently split to form two molecules of pyruvic **acid**. This enzyme-controlled pathway is confined to the cytoplasm of **the** cell. It is described in Figures 3.1 and 3.2.

As the skeleton diagram (Figure 3.2) shows, there are eight **main** reactions in this pathway.

Reaction 1

In this reaction a phosphate group ($-PO_3^{2-}$) is added to the glucose molecule. The glucose has been **phosphorylated**. The phosphate group is provided by the hydrolysis of an ATP molecule in the presence of a phosphorylase enzyme (*hexokinase*).

> **Why is the product called glucose-6-phosphate?**

The phosphate group is attached to the hydroxyl group (OH) of carbon atom number 6 of the glucose molecule. In bonding to the phosphate group a hydrogen ion (H^+) is liberated as well as a molecule of **ADP.**

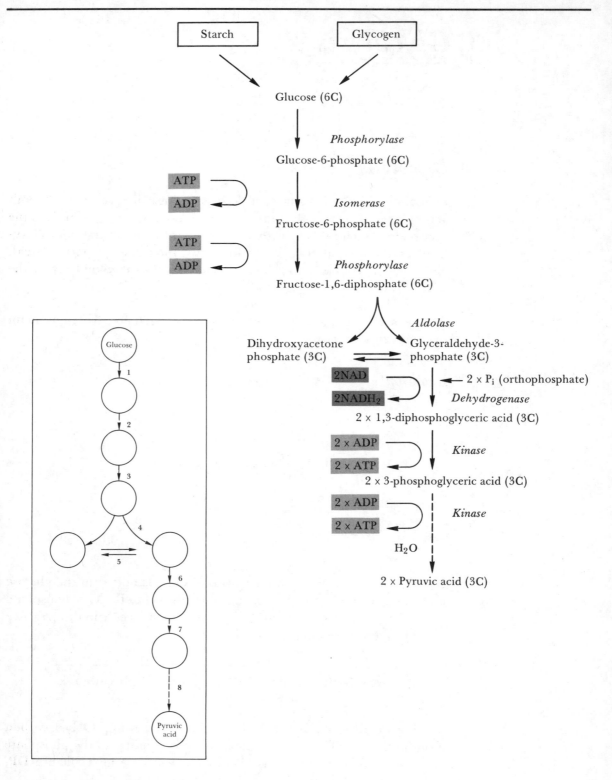

Starch

Glycogen

Glucose (6C)

Phosphorylase

Glucose-6-phosphate (6C)

ATP

ADP

Isomerase

Fructose-6-phosphate (6C)

ATP

ADP

Phosphorylase

Fructose-1,6-diphosphate (6C)

Aldolase

Dihydroxyacetone phosphate (3C)

Glyceraldehyde-3-phosphate (3C)

2NAD

2NADH$_2$

← 2 × P$_i$ (orthophosphate)

Dehydrogenase

2 × 1,3-diphosphoglyceric acid (3C)

2 × ADP

2 × ATP

Kinase

2 × 3-phosphoglyceric acid (3C)

2 × ADP

2 × ATP

Kinase

H$_2$O

2 × Pyruvic acid (3C)

Glucose

1

2

3

4

5

6

7

8

Pyruvic acid

Figure 3.2 *Skeleton diagram of the glycolytic pathway*

Reaction 2

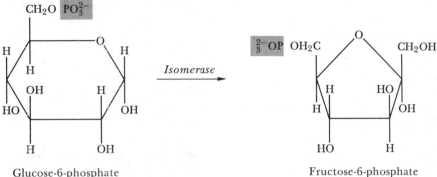

Glucose-6-phosphate   Fructose-6-phosphate

The six-membered pyranose ring of glucose-6-phosphate is converted into the five-membered furanose ring of fructose-6-phosphate. This reaction is basically a molecular rearrangement – no groups have been added or removed. Such a reaction is called **isomerisation** and is catalysed by an isomerase enzyme (*phosphoglucose isomerase*).

It is not necessary at this level to consider the actual mechanism involved in the isomerisation.

Reaction 3

Fructose-6-phosphate   Fructose-1,6-diphosphate

Following the isomerisation reaction fructose-6-phosphate is phosphorylated to fructose-1,6-diphosphate. As with reaction 1 the phosphate group is provided by the hydrolysis of an ATP molecule. The phosphorylation is carried out by a phosphorylase enzyme (*phosphofructokinase*) and again results in the production of a molecule of ADP and a hydrogen ion (H^+).

> ## Why 1,6-diphosphate?

The first phosphate group was attached to carbon atom number 6; the second is attached to carbon atom number 1. 'Di' refers to the fact that there are now two separate phosphate groups, thus we have fructose-1, 6-diphosphate.

Reaction 4

Fructose-1,6-diphosphate

Fructose-1,6-diphosphate is shown in its open chain form in order to show the essentials of this reaction.

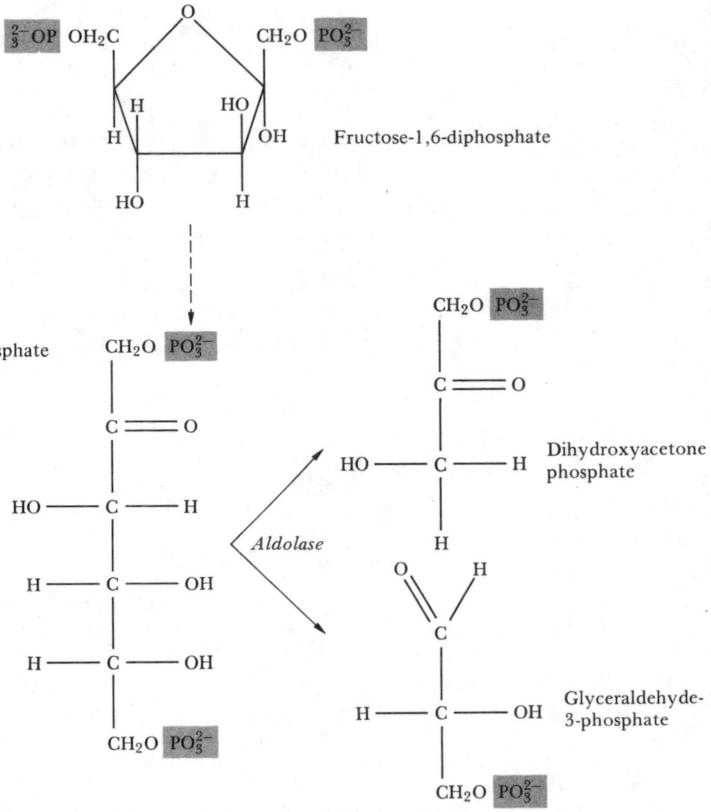

Aldolase

Dihydroxyacetone phosphate

Glyceraldehyde-3-phosphate

In this reaction fructose-1,6-diphosphate is split by an aldolase enzyme into two interconvertible (by isomerisation) phosphorylated 3C (three-carbon) units. For convenience these two compounds are often referred to as **triose phosphates**.

Reaction 5

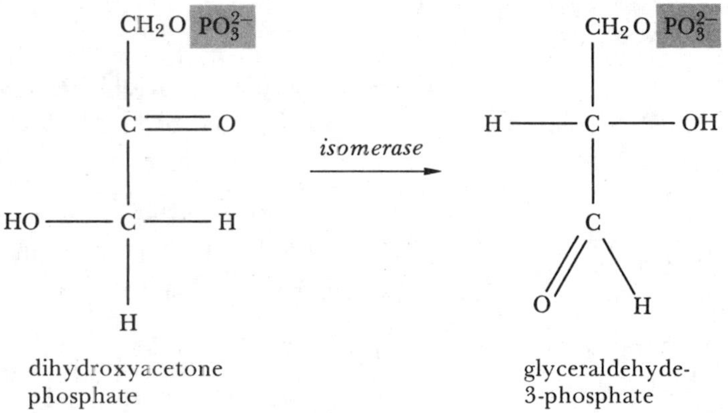

dihydroxyacetone phosphate   →   glyceraldehyde-3-phosphate

This is the isomeric interconversion of dihydroxyacetone phosphate to glyceraldehyde-3-phosphate by another isomerase enzyme (*triose phosphate isomerase*).

Why is dihydroxyacetone phosphate converted to glyceraldehyde-3-phosphate?

This is necessary because glyceraldehyde-3-phosphate is more readily converted to pyruvic acid, so the conversion ensures that both parts of the fructose-1,6-diphosphate are utilised.

Note: All the reactions beyond this point occur twice because a single glucose molecule generates two molecules of triose phosphate.

Reaction 6

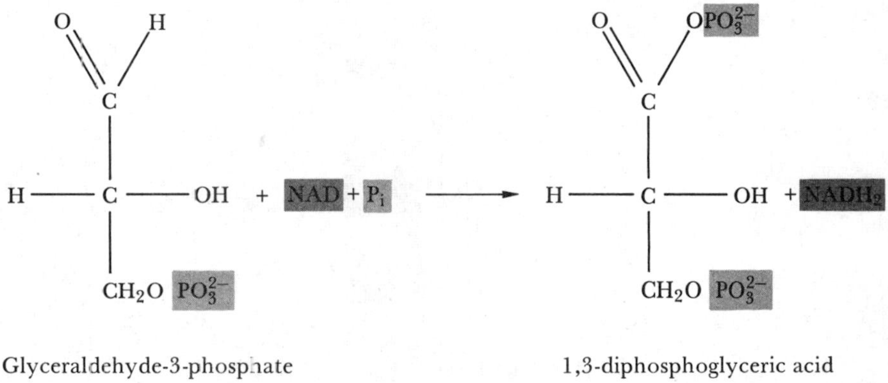

Glyceraldehyde-3-phosphate   1,3-diphosphoglyceric acid

Glyceraldehyde-3-phosphate is oxidised and phosphorylated to 1, 3-diphosphoglyceric acid.

> **How is glyceraldehyde-3-phosphate oxidised and phosphorylated at the same time?**

P_i (inorganic phosphate) represents orthophosphate (HPO_4^{2-}), found within living cells. It is a stable ion formed from phosphoric acid (H_3PO_4) and is responsible for this oxidation and phosphorylation as shown below.

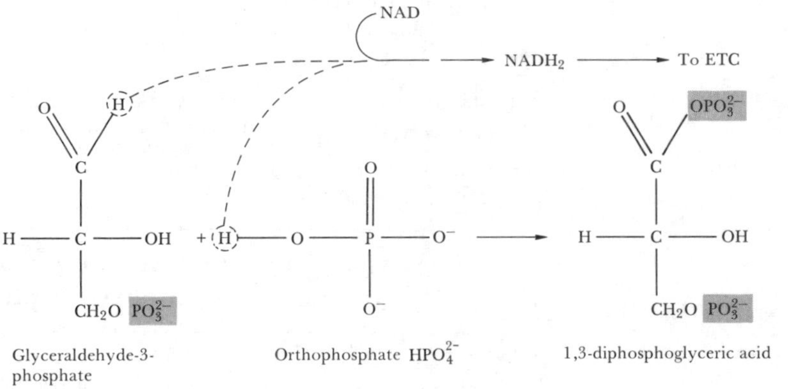

Glyceraldehyde-3-phosphate   Orthophosphate HPO_4^{2-} 1,3-diphosphoglyceric acid

The orthophosphate combines with the glyceraldehyde-3-phosphate, releasing two hydrogen atoms which are accepted by the hydrogen carrier nicotinamide adenine dinucleotide (NAD) which is reduced in the process (to $NADH_2$). The $NADH_2$ then carries these hydrogen atoms into a mitochondrion where they enter the electron transfer chain (see chapter 5.) The glyceraldehyde-3-phosphate has been oxidised because it has lost a hydrogen atom and gained an oxygen atom.

Reaction 7

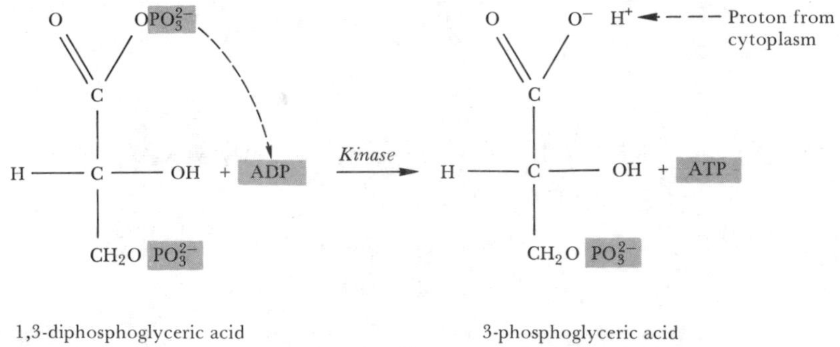

1,3-diphosphoglyceric acid   3-phosphoglyceric acid

Up until reaction 7, glycolysis has resulted in the consumption of two molecules of ATP. This reaction is the first to generate ATP. The kinase enzyme *phosphoglycerate kinase* catalyses the removal of the phosphate from carbon atom number 1 and its direct combination with ADP to form ATP.

You will remember that certain reactions are **exothermic** – they liberate energy. Reaction 7 can be looked upon as an exothermic reaction in which the release of energy is directly coupled to ATP synthesis via the kinase enzyme, rather than being lost as heat and light.

Reaction 8

3-phosphoglyceric acid   Proton from cytoplasm   Pyruvic acid

This reaction summarises a series of reactions during which the second phosphate group is removed and combined with ADP to form another molecule of ATP. In addition, the 3-phosphoglyceric acid is dehydrated, releasing a molecule of water.

The fate of the pyruvic acid now depends upon whether oxygen is available. If it is, the pyruvic acid is completely oxidised in the mitochondrion to carbon dioxide and water (aerobic respiration). If it is not, the pyruvic acid will be converted into ethanol or lactic acid (anaerobic respiration).

Summary of glycolysis

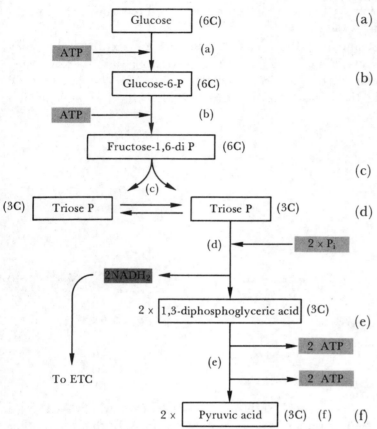

Figure 3.3   *Summary of glycolysis*

(a)   Glucose is phosphorylated to glucose-6-phosphate. One ATP is used up.

(b)   Glucose-6-phosphate undergoes isomerisation followed by further phosphorylation to form fructose-1,6-diphosphate. A second ATP is used up.

(c)   Fructose-1,6-diphosphate is split into two 3C triose phosphates.

(d)   Both triose phosphates are oxidised (removal of H_2) and phosphorylated by addition of orthophosphate (P_i) forming two molecules of 1,3-diphosphoglyceric acid.

(e)   1,3-diphosphoglyceric acids undergo a series of reactions in which their phosphate groups are removed to produce a total of four ATP molecules.

(f)   The final product of glycolysis is one molecule of pyruvic acid per 1,3-diphosphoglyceric acid or in other words two molecules of pyruvic acid for every glucose molecule.

Revision points

1 Glycolysis is the first stage of cellular respiration and is common to both aerobic and anaerobic respiration.

2 It takes place in the cytoplasm of the cell.

3 Two ATP molecules are consumed in the initial phosphorylation reactions and a molecule of orthophosphate is required in the subsequent phosphorylation of each of the triose phosphates.

4 Four ATP molecules are produced during the final conversion of the 1,3-diphosphoglyceric acids into pyruvic acids.

5 There is therefore a net gain of two ATP molecules per glucose molecule.

6 In addition four atoms of hydrogen are liberated in the oxidation/phosphorylation of triose phosphate (reaction 6). These are accepted by two molecules of NAD and transported to the electron transfer chain as $NADH_2$ (see chapter 5.)

7 Two molecules of pyruvic acid are produced for every molecule of glucose that enters the pathway.

8 The overall strategy behind glycolysis is the formation of three carbon units (pyruvic acid) which are easily able to enter the Krebs cycle (see chapter 4).

4 Krebs cycle (tricarboxylic acid cycle)

Krebs cycle

The potential energy yield for one molecule of glucose in aerobic respiration is 38 molecules of ATP.

Glycolysis has produced only two molecules of ATP – so 36 molecules of ATP must still be 'locked up' inside the pyruvic acid molecules. In order for this energy to be released the pyruvic acid enters a complex series of reactions collectively termed the **Krebs cycle**, after its discoverer Sir Hans Krebs. The reactions are known alternatively as the **citric acid cycle**, since the first intermediate formed from pyruvic acid is citric acid, or the **tricarboxylic acid cycle** (TCA cycle) as some of the intermediates are tricarboxylic acids (they have three COOH groups each). This cyclical pathway occurs in the matrix of the mitochondrion.

> **How does pyruvic acid enter the Krebs cycle?**

When oxygen is available pyruvic acid combines with a compound called coenzyme A (CoA) to form **acetyl coenzyme A (acetyl CoA).** This reaction is catalysed by a large multienzyme complex and involves an **oxidative decarboxylation** reaction. Oxidation is the removal of hydrogen and decarboxylation the removal of carbon dioxide.

The overall reaction can be summarised as follows:

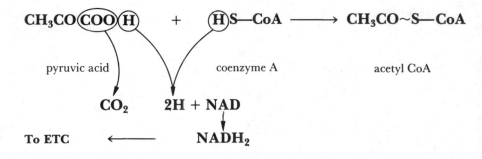

HS: terminal sulphydryl group attached to CoA
~: energy-rich bond

Acetyl CoA is now able to enter the Krebs cycle by combining with the four-carbon compound oxaloacetic acid to form citric acid (6C). The energy for this reaction is provided by the hydrolysis of the energy-rich bond linking CoA to the acetyl group.

Coenzyme A is a universal carrier of acetyl groups and provides the main entry point into the Krebs cycle. Once it has deposited its acetyl group ($CH_3 CO$) with oxaloacetic acid it is free to pick up another pyruvic acid, as shown below:

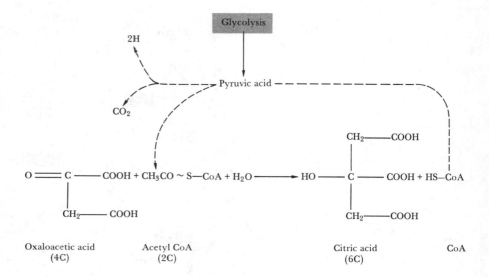

The citric acid (6C) now undergoes a series of enzyme-mediated decarboxylations and dehydrogenations until oxaloacetic acid is regenerated, and the cycle repeats itself. All these reactions are carried out by dehydrogenase and decarboxylase enzymes.

> **Since citric acid is eventually converted back to oxaloacetic acid what does the cycle achieve?**

The answer to this lies in the repeated dehydrogenations of the cycle's intermediates. One complete revolution of the cycle liberates four pairs of hydrogen atoms which are accepted by NAD or FAD and transported to the electron transfer chain where they are used in the generation of ATP (see chapter 5).

The Krebs cycle is shown in Figures 4.1 and 4.2.

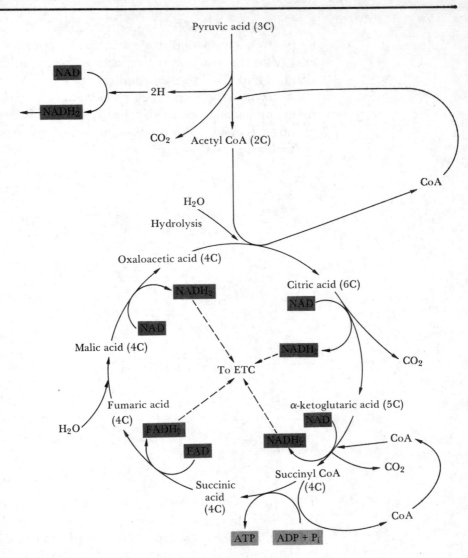

Figure 4.1 *Krebs cycle (simplified)*

As the skeleton diagram (Figure 4.2) indicates, the Krebs cycle can be split into six main reactions.

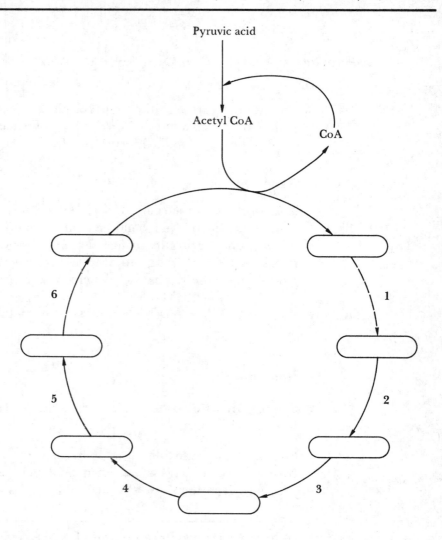

———— Broken lines indicate stages where intermediates have been omitted

Figure 4.2   *Skeleton diagram of Krebs cycle*

Reaction 1

citric acid ⟶ **isocitric acid** ⟶ **α-ketoglutaric acid + CO$_2$ + 2H**

   (6C)   (6C)   (5C)

The citric acid undergoes an oxidative decarboxylation releasing one molecule of carbon dioxide and two hydrogen atoms. To allow this to take place citric acid is first isomerized to isocitric acid (6C).

Reaction 2

$$\alpha\text{-ketoglutaric acid } + \text{ HS—CoA} \longrightarrow \text{ succinyl}\sim\text{S—CoA } + CO_2 + 2H$$

| (5C) | coenzyme A | succinyl coenzyme A (4C) |

Oxidative decarboxylation of α-ketoglutaric acid and its combination with CoA results in the production of succinyl CoA. Again one molecule of carbon dioxide and two hydrogen atoms are released.

Reaction 3

The formation of succinyl CoA is important at this stage because it contains an energy-rich bond (similar to that of acetyl CoA). Cleavage of this bond during the conversion of succinyl CoA to succinic acid releases sufficient energy to generate a molecule of ATP. This is the only stage in the Krebs cycle where ATP is generated directly.

$$\text{succinyl}\sim\text{S—CoA } + P_i + \text{ADP} \longrightarrow \text{ succinic acid } + \text{ATP } + \text{HS—CoA}$$

(4C)   (4C)

Reaction 4

$$\text{succinic acid } \longrightarrow \text{ fumaric acid } + 2H$$

(4C)   (4C)

Succinic acid is oxidised to fumaric acid by the removal of two hydrogen atoms. This is the only dehydrogenation in the cycle in which the hydrogen atoms are accepted by FAD instead of NAD.

Why is FAD used here instead of NAD as the hydrogen acceptor?

Both NAD and FAD are associated with the dehydrogenase enzymes of the cycle. Once NAD has accepted two hydrogen atoms it leaves its dehydrogenase enzymes and transports them to the electron transfer chain (see chapter 5). FAD, however, is a prosthetic group and consequently is tightly bound to *succinic acid dehydrogenase*, the enzyme responsible the dehydrogenation at this stage.

Succinic acid dehydrogenase is the only enzyme of the Krebs cycle that forms part of the inner mitochondrial membrane. It is thus intimately associated with the membrane proteins making up the electron transfer chain and as a result provides a direct entry point into the electron transfer chain for the hydrogen atoms released by the dehydrogenation of succinic acid. The use of NAD as a means of transporting the hydrogen atoms to the electron transport chain is therefore negated in this reaction.

Reaction 5

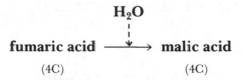

$$H_2O$$

fumaric acid $\longrightarrow$ malic acid

(4C)   (4C)

Fumaric acid undergoes hydration (incorporation of H_2O) followed by isomerisation to form malic acid.

Reaction 6

malic acid $\longrightarrow$ oxaloacetic acid + 2H

(4C)   (4C)

The final reaction of the cycle regenerates oxaloacetic acid by the dehydrogenation of malic acid.

The products of glycolysis and the Krebs cycle

For every acetyl CoA molecule that enters the Krebs cycle the products are:

(a) **2 molecules of carbon dioxide**
(b) **1 molecule of ATP**
(c) **4 pairs of hydrogen atoms.**

Since two molecules of acetyl CoA are produced for every glucose molecule the Krebs cycle must rotate twice per glucose molecule oxidised. The net products of the Krebs cycle for a single glucose molecule are therefore:

(a) **4 molecules of carbon dioxide**
(b) **2 molecules of ATP**
(c) **8 pairs of hydrogen atoms.**

In addition the oxidative decarboxylation of the two pyruvic acids which link glycolysis to the Krebs cycle results in the production of:

(a) **2 pairs of hydrogen atoms**
(b) **2 molecules of carbon dioxide.**

Up until this stage only four ATP molecules have been generated directly: two in glycolysis and two in the Krebs cycle. The remaining 34 ATPs are generated by the passage of the hydrogen atoms through the electron transfer chain. A total of 12 pairs of hydrogen atoms have been released per glucose molecule.

Glycolysis

$$(2 \times 2H) + 2NAD \longrightarrow 2NADH_2$$

Link stage

$$(2 \times 2H) + 2NAD \longrightarrow 2NADH_2$$

Krebs cycle

$$(6 \times 2H) + 6NAD \longrightarrow 6NADH_2$$

$$(2 \times 2H) + 2FAD \longrightarrow 2FADH_2$$

$$\text{total} = 10\ NADH_2 + 2FADH_2$$

These 12 pairs of hydrogen atoms generate sufficient energy for the production of the remaining 34 ATPs (see chapter 5).

What happens to the carbon dioxide released by the decarboxylations?

The six molecules of carbon dioxide diffuse out of the cell and are expired.

$$C_6H_{12}O_6 + 6O_2 \longrightarrow \text{energy} + 6H_2O + \boxed{6CO_2}$$

Summary of the Krebs cycle

The detailed diagram and explanations provided in this chapter are not meant to be reproduced under exam conditions! The summary diagram (Figure 4.3) and notes are supplied for this purpose.

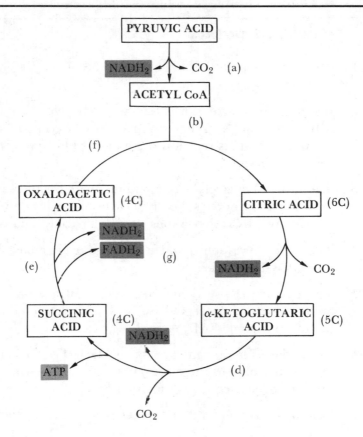

Figure 4.3 *Summary of Krebs cycle*

(a) Pyruvic acid (3C) undergoes oxidative decarboxylation and combination with coenzyme A to form acetyl coenzyme A (2C).

(b) Acetyl CoA combines with oxaloacetic acid (4C) to form citric acid (6C). CoA returns to 'pick up' another pyruvic acid molecule.

(c) Citric acid undergoes oxidative decarboxylation to form α-ketoglutaric acid (5C).

(d) α-ketoglutaric acid undergoes another oxidative decarboxylation to form succinic acid (4C). Sufficient energy is released in this reaction to generate one molecule of ATP directly.

(e) Succinic acid is converted into oxaloacetic acid in three steps (oxidation–hydration–oxidation) releasing two pairs of hydrogen atoms. One pair is accepted by FAD.

(f) Oxaloacetic acid is now ready to combine with another molecule of acetyl CoA and the cycle repeats itself (twice for every glucose molecule).

(g) The pairs of hydrogen atoms released are transported to the electron transfer chain by hydrogen carriers (NAD or FAD).

Revision points

1   The reactions of the Krebs cycle occur in the matrix of the mitochondrion.

2   Before pyruvic acid can enter the Krebs cycle it must first react with coenzyme A in an oxidative decarboxylation to form acetyl coenzyme A. This reaction represents a link stage between glycolysis and the Krebs cycle.

3   The two-carbon acetyl CoA combines with the four-carbon oxaloacetic acid to form the six-carbon citric acid. This undergoes a series of oxidative decarboxylations until oxaloacetic acid is regenerated.

4   The decarboxylations remove carbon dioxide molecules which will ultimately be exhaled.

5   The oxidations (by dehydrogenation) release pairs of hydrogen atoms which are accepted by NAD. At one stage an alternative hydrogen carrier, FAD, is used.

6   The reduced hydrogen carriers ($NADH_2$/$FADH_2$) transport their hydrogen atoms to the electron transfer chain where they will be used in the subsequent generation of ATP.

7   One molecule of ATP is generated directly for each turn of the cycle.

8   The cycle of reactions rotates twice per glucose molecule oxidised.

9   The link stage and the Krebs cycle together produce: 2 molecules of ATP, 10 pairs of hydrogen atoms and 6 molecules of carbon dioxide for every glucose molecule oxidised.

10 The Krebs cycle is not concerned solely with the oxidation of carbohydrate. Fats and proteins are also oxidised in this way and most enter the cycle as two-carbon acetyl groups via acetyl CoA.

11 Consequently acetyl CoA is a molecule of major biochemical importance common to the oxidation of most foods.

5 *The electron transfer chain (ETC) (the respiratory chain)*

The electron transfer chain

Up until this stage respiration has been geared almost entirely to the production of reduced hydrogen carriers ($NADH_2$ or $FADH_2$). The significance of this is that each $NADH_2$ molecule releases sufficient energy to produce three molecules of ATP when reoxidised to NAD. ($FADH_2$ only releases enough energy to produce two ATP molecules; the reason for this will become clear later!)

During the series of reactions that comprise the **electron transfer chain** (**ETC**), $NADH_2$ donates high-energy electrons which are passed along a series of carrier molecules before finally combining with an oxygen atom (O) to form water. The movement of these electrons results in the pumping of protons and the subsequent synthesis of ATP.

The carriers include three large multienzyme protein complexes: **NADH dehydrogenase**, **cytochrome reductase** and **cytochrome oxidase**, and two smaller electron carriers **ubiquinone** (sometimes called **coenzyme Q**) and **cytochrome C**.

Where in the mitochrondrion are these carriers found?

They are components of the inner mitochondrial membrane. The multienzyme complexes are globular proteins which span the lipid bilayer.

If NAD carries hydrogen atoms, where do the high-energy electrons come from?

As explained in chapter 1 NAD carries its hydrogens separately as protons and electrons:

$$NAD^+ + \underbrace{2H^+ + 2e^-}_{\text{2 H atoms}} \longrightarrow \underbrace{NADH + H^+}_{NADH_2 \text{ (reduced)}}$$

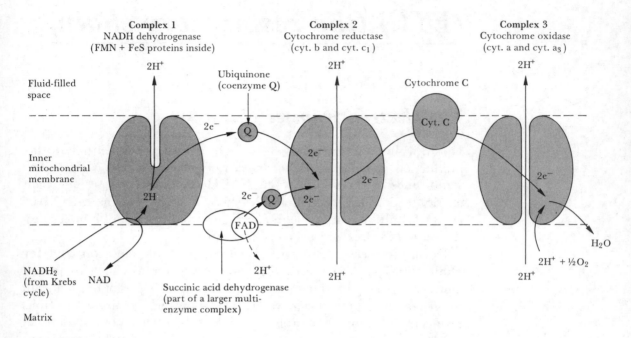

Figure 5.1   *The electron transfer chain*

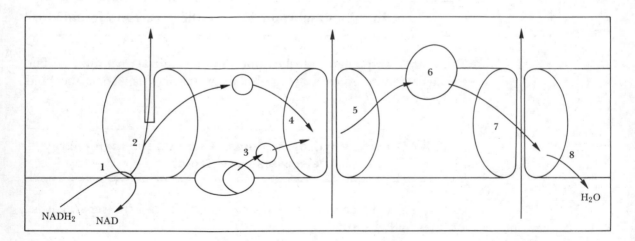

Figure 5.2   *Skeleton diagram of the electron transfer chain*

When the $NADH_2$ is reoxidised the hydrogens are released as protons and high-energy electrons:

$$\textbf{NADH}_2 \longrightarrow \textbf{NAD}^+ + \textbf{2H}^+ + \textbf{2e}^-$$

high-energy
electrons

These are the electrons which are passed along the chain of carrier molecules. The way in which their energy is used will be discussed shortly.

Figures 5.1 and 5.2 show the structure of the ETC in more detail.

Although this appears very complicated, there are basically eight stages involved, as the skeleton diagram (Figure 5.2) indicates.

Reaction 1

$NADH_2$ releases its hydrogen atoms which are accepted by the prosthetic group **FMN (flavine mononucleotide)** of the enzyme *NADH dehydrogenase*, the first carrier of the chain:

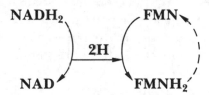

In this reaction the FMN is simply acting as another hydrogen acceptor by taking the two hydrogen atoms from the $NADH_2$. This now means the NAD is free to act as a hydrogen acceptor again – it has been reoxidised. By accepting the hydrogen atoms FMN itself is reduced (to $FMNH_2$). In some texts the whole of complex 1 is referred to as **flavoprotein**.

Reaction 2

As mentioned earlier, the two hydrogen atoms comprise two protons ($2 H^+$) and two electrons ($2 e^-$).

The electrons are passed on to a series of **iron–sulphur proteins** which form the second prosthetic group of NAD dehydrogenase. These iron–sulphur proteins now pass the electrons on to the second carrier, **ubiquinone (coenzyme Q)**.

But what happens to the protons?

They are ejected into the fluid-filled space between the two mitochondrial membranes.

Reaction 3

As you will recall from chapter 4 FAD is unusual in that it is a prosthetic group and so remains associated with the Krebs cycle enzyme *succinic acid dehydrogenase*. This enzyme is a constituent of the inner mitochondrial membrane. Consequently FAD is able to donate electrons directly to ubiquinone. $NADH_2$ is unable to do this because it is not directly associated with a membrane-bound protein. The remaining protons are released into the mitochondrial matrix:

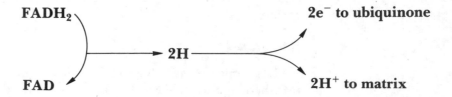

Again this frees FAD to accept more hydrogens.

It is worth noting at this point that $FADH_2$ has entered the electron transfer chain at a stage after the first two protons have been deposited into the intermembrane space. The significance of this will be explained later.

Reaction 4

The electron carrier ubiquinone is thought to be extremely mobile within the fluid lipid bilayer of the membrane. There may be up to 10 times as much ubiquinone present compared with the other carriers. Molecules of ubiquinone carrying their electrons float at random through the fluid bilayer until they collide with one of the many protein complexes that serve as the second complex, *cytochrome reductase*.

Reaction 5

Complex 2, cytochrome reductase, is made up of cytochromes b and c_1. All cytochrome molecules possess a central metal ion. They belong to a group of chemicals called **porphyrins**. In the case of cytochrome b the metal ion is iron (Fe^{2+}). Like other metallic elements iron reacts to achieve a more stable state by losing electrons. In practice it does this by losing either two or three electrons to form Fe^{2+} or Fe^{3+} ions. In the

Fe^{2+} ion there are two more protons in the nucleus than there are electrons surrounding the nucleus. The overall result is a net 2+ charge. Similarly Fe^{3+} ions have lost three electrons to produce a net 3+ charge. It is the ability of iron to convert from one of these two major ions to the other (depending upon conditions) that allows cytochromes to act as electron carriers.

The electrons are now accepted from ubiquinone by the iron(III) ions at the centre of the cytochromes:

$$e^- + Fe^{3+} \longrightarrow Fe^{2+}$$

The iron(III) ion, Fe^{3+}, gained an electron and is therefore said to be reduced to Fe^{2+} (oxidation is loss of electrons).

Clearly a cytochrome is only able to accept one electron at a time – it is therefore thought that ubiquinone passes one of its electrons on to cytochrome b and the other to cytochrome c_1:

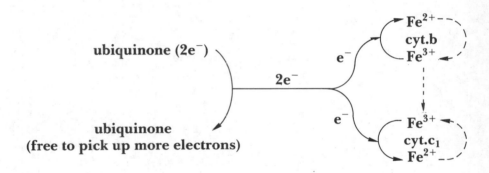

Note: This reaction has been greatly simplified for ease of understanding. In fact cytochrome b serves as a temporary electron store, passing its electron on to cytochrome c_1 when cytochrome c_1 has lost the first electron.

The movement of the two high-energy electrons through complex 2 provides the energy required to open a proton channel through the complex, allowing two protons (H^+) to be pumped across the membrane from the matrix to the fluid-filled intermembrane space.

Reaction 6

Cytochrome c_1 (complex 2) passes two electrons on to the next carrier, **cytochrome C**. This carrier is found embedded in the outside surface of the membrane, projecting into the intermembrane space.

Cytochrome C then transfers the two electrons to the final carrier complex, *cytochrome oxidase*.

Reaction 7

Cytochrome oxidase (complex 3) also consists of two cytochromes, a and a_3. Again the passage of electrons through these cytochromes provides the energy required to open a proton channel, allowing a final two protons to be pumped across the membrane.

> ## What happens to the electrons when they reach the end of the chain?

Cytochrome oxidase also catalyses the following reaction:

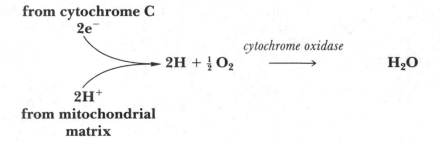

The two electrons combine with two protons to form two hydrogen atoms (2H), which are then passed on to an oxygen atom to form water. This water passes into the matrix where some of it may be used in the reactions of the Krebs cycle.

As you can see, oxygen serves as the final acceptor for hydrogen. Without oxygen, therefore, the electron transfer chain will not function. Imagine it like this: the ETC is a conveyer belt passing electrons along its length with oxygen waiting at the far end to remove them. Unless they are removed in this way the electrons accumulate at the end, causing the belt to grind to a halt.

> ## What would happen if the ETC stopped?

Without the ETC all the reduced coenzyme ($NADH_2$/$FADH_2$) produced in glycolysis and the Krebs cycle cannot be reoxidised. Eventually all the coenzyme (NAD/FAD) in the cell will be in the reduced form and therefore unable to accept any further hydrogen atoms. At this point the Krebs cycle would also grind to a halt since there would be nothing to remove the hydrogen atoms produced during the oxidative decarboxylation reactions that are taking place (see chapter 4). This is in fact what happens in anaerobic respiration – the ETC and

Krebs cycle cannot function. In other words, anaerobic respiration consists of glycolysis only (see chapter 7).

You will remember that electrons from $NADH_2$ travel the full length of the ETC causing six protons to be pumped into the fluid-filled intermembrane space of the mitochondrion. Those from $FADH_2$, however, enter after the first pumping stage so only cause four protons to be pumped across.

> ## What is the significance of this proton pumping?

It is the controlled flow of these protons back across the membrane into the matrix that drives the synthesis of ATP (according to the chemiosmotic theory – see chapter 6). Each pair of protons generates sufficient energy to synthesise one molecule of ATP. This process will be fully explained in the next chapter. As a consequence of this the oxidation of one molecule of $NADH_2$ provides three molecules of ATP while the oxidation of one $FADH_2$ molecule only provides two molecules of ATP.

Summary of the electron transfer chain

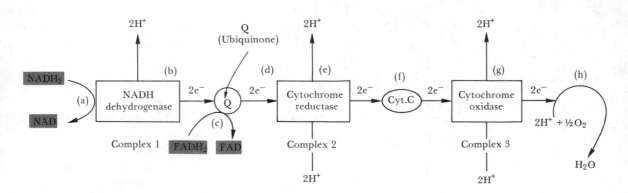

Figure 5.3   *Summary of the electron transfer chain*

(a) $NADH_2$ donates hydrogen atoms ($2H^+ + 2e^-$) to NADH dehydrogenase (carrier 1).

(b)   The hydrogen atoms' protons are ejected into the intermembrane space and its electrons are passed on to ubiquinone (carrier 2).

(c)   Ubiquinone carriers can also pick up electrons from $FADH_2$.

(d)   Mobile ubiquinone carriers transfer their electrons to cytochrome reductase (carrier 3).

(e)   Movement of electrons through the cytochrome reductase complex facilitates the pumping of two more protons into the intermembrane space.

(f)   Cytochrome C (carrier 4) accepts electrons from cytochrome reductase and transfers them to the fifth carrier, cytochrome oxidase.

(g)   The movement of electrons through the cytochrome oxidase complex again facilitates the pumping of a final pair of protons into the intermembrane space.

(h)   The electrons finally combine with protons from the matrix to form hydrogen atoms which reduce molecular oxygen to water. This reaction is catalysed by cytochrome oxidase.

Revision points

1   The ETC consists of a chain of at least five carrier molecules, **NADH dehydrogenase**, **ubiquinone**, **cytochrome reductase**, **cytochrome C**, and **cytochrome oxidase**.

2   The components of the chain float in the lipid bilayer of the inner mitochondrial membrane.

3   Hydrogen atoms are supplied to the chain by either $NADH_2$ or $FADH_2$ (as protons and electrons).

4   The hydrogen atoms' electrons are passed along the chain by a series of random collisions between the carriers.

5   The carriers are alternately reduced and oxidised as the electrons are transferred from one carrier to the next. As a result the reactions of the ETC are termed **redox** (**red**uction/**ox**idation) reactions.

6   Three of the five carriers are large protein complexes which span the membrane and act as proton pumps. Two protons are pumped into the intermembrane space every time two electrons pass through each complex. The other two are mobile electron carriers linking the three complexes.

7   If $NADH_2$ supplies the hydrogens, six protons are pumped across the membrane. If $FADH_2$ supplies the hydrogens, only four protons are pumped across. This is because $FADH_2$ enters the chain at a point after the first proton pump.

8   The movement of protons across the membrane back into the matrix drives ATP synthesis. Every two protons generate one molecule of ATP, so each molecule of $NADH_2$ generates three ATPs. Each $FADH_2$ generates only two ATPs.

9   Oxygen serves as the final acceptor at the end of the chain, combining with reconstituted hydrogen atoms to form water.

10   The reactions of the ETC are often referred to as **oxidative phosphorylation**. The reason for this is that $NADH_2$ and $FADH_2$ are oxidised (by removal of hydrogen) and this oxidation is coupled to ATP synthesis. ATP is synthesised by a phosphorylation reaction – hence oxidative phosphorylation.

6 The synthesis of ATP

The synthesis of ATP (including chemiosmosis)

As already outlined in chapter 5, the flow of electrons along the carriers of the ETC causes protons (H^+) to be pumped across the inner mitochondrial membrane. This establishes a high concentration of protons in the fluid-filled space between the two mitochondrial membranes, as shown in Figure 6.1.

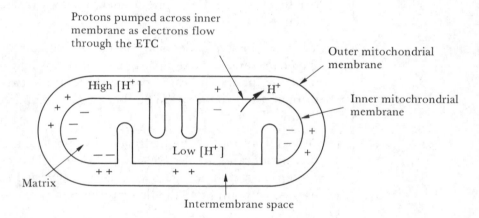

Protons pumped across inner membrane as electrons flow through the ETC

Outer mitochondrial membrane

Inner mitochrondrial membrane

High [H^+]

H^+

Low [H^+]

Matrix

Intermembrane space

Figure 6.1 *ETC carriers pump electrons across the inner mitochondrial membrane into the matrix*

This proton gradient across the inner mitochondrial membrane is a store of free energy, since the flow of protons back through the membrane drives the synthesis of ATP. The hydroelectric power station shown in Figure 6.2 provides a useful analogy of this process.

This coupling of electron transfer/proton pumping with ATP synthesis was proposed by Peter Mitchell (1961) in his **chemiosmotic hypothesis**. The potential energy stored in the proton gradient created by the ETC has two components:

(a)   A difference in chemical concentration of protons. Proton concentration is another term for pH, so in other words there is a pH gradient across the membrane (a difference of 1.4 pH units).

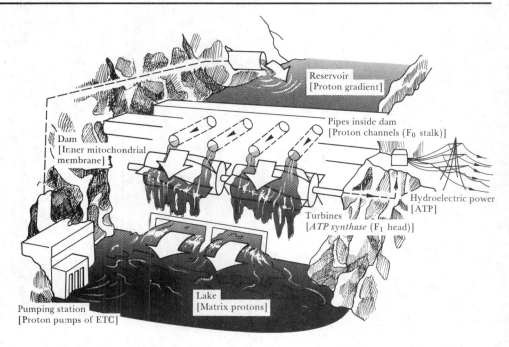

Reservoir
[Proton gradient]

Pipes inside dam
[Proton channels (F_0 stalk)]

Dam
[Inner mitochondrial
membrane]

Hydroelectric power
[ATP]

Turbines
[*ATP synthase* (F_1 head)]

Pumping station
[Proton pumps of ETC]

Lake
[Matrix protons]

Figure 6.2   *The flow of protons drives the synthesis of ATP, as the flow of water through turbines produces hydroelectric power*

(b)   A difference in electric potential. All protons carry an electric charge ($+1$) so the excess of protons in the intermembrane space causes the difference in electric potential across the membrane (approximately 140 millivolts).

There is therefore a tendency for the protons to diffuse back into the matrix down this **electrochemical gradient**. Since the inner mitochrondrial membrane must be impermeable to protons in order to maintain this gradient, this diffusion can only occur through specialised proton channels.

> ### Where are these proton channels?

Electron micrographs of the inner mitochondrial membrane show the matrix surface to be studded with numerous globular projections. These consist of a protein head called the **F_1 unit**, and a protein stalk called the **F_0 unit**. The F_0 unit is embedded in and spans the membrane. It is these F_0 stalks that function as the proton channels.

> ### How does the flow of protons drive ATP synthesis?

The F_1 head of each stalked particle is in fact an ATP synthase enzyme. The passage of two protons through this enzyme from the F_0 channel causes a molecule of ADP to be phosphorylated to ATP, as shown by Figure 6.3.

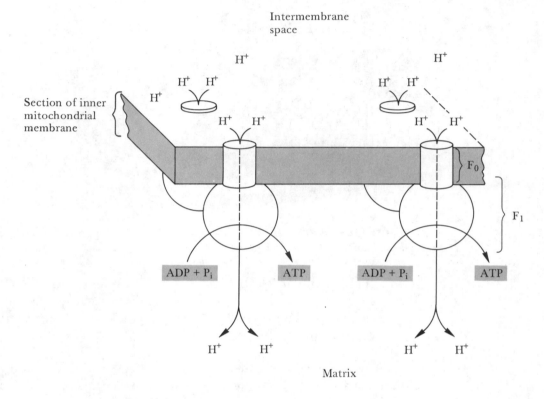

Figure 6.3   *The phosphorylation of ADP to ATP*

The exact mechanism of ATP synthesis at the active site of the F_1 head is still unclear. There are however two main theories, **direct** and **indirect phosphorylation**.

Direct phosphorylation

As protons move from the F_0 channel into the active site of the ATP synthase they bind with one of the oxygens from a phosphate group to form water. This enables the phosphate to bond with ADP forming ATP. The ATP molecule then detaches from the enzyme.

Indirect phosphorylation

Evidence indicates that ADP and P_i can combine spontaneously once in the active site of the ATP synthase, although the ATP molecule formed in this way remains tightly bound to the enzyme. The flow of charged protons through the F_1 head is thought to produce a conformational change in the enzyme's active site sufficient to release the ATP.

Experiments have since shown that ATP synthase can make ATP in the absence of proton flow. This would tend to support the second hypothesis that suggests proton flow has a more indirect role in ATP production **by releasing tightly bound ATP from the enzyme's active site**, instead of driving its production directly.

The energy budget for the complete oxidation of a single glucose molecule

Table 6.1 *The ATP produced at each stage*

Stage	NAD/FAD	ATP
Glycolysis (cytoplasm)		
(a) Phosphorylations of glucose and fructose-6-phosphate		−2
(b) Conversion of triose phosphates to 1, 3-diphosphoglyceric acids	$2 \times NADH_2 \longrightarrow$	+6
(c) Conversion of 1, 3-diphosphoglyceric acids to pyruvic acids		+4
Link stage (mitochondrial matrix)		
(d) Conversion of pyruvic acids to acetyl CoAs	$2 \times NADH_2 \longrightarrow$	+6
Krebs cycle (mitochondrial matrix)		
(e) Oxidative decarboxylations of citric acid through to oxaloacetic acid	$6 \times NADH_2 \longrightarrow$ $2 \times FADH_2 \longrightarrow$	+18 +4
(f) Conversion of succinyl CoA to succinic acid		+2
	Total: 38 ATPs	

The problem with cytoplasmic NADH₂

The vast majority of ATP produced in respiration is generated by the reoxidation of reduced coenzyme (NADH₂/FADH₂) via the ETC. This is easily accomplished since most of the reduced coenzyme only has to transport its hydrogen atoms from the Krebs cycle enzymes in the matrix to the carriers of the ETC located within the inner mitochondrial membrane. A problem arises, however, with the two molecules of NADH₂ produced by glycolysis in the cytoplasm of the cell. The outer mitochondrial membrane, like the inner membrane bounding the matrix, is impermeable (this is necessary to maintain the chemiosmotic proton gradient). This problem is overcome by shuttling the electrons from NADH₂ across the membrane, rather than moving the NADH₂ itself. This is achieved by means of two different membrane-bound shuttle systems.

The glycerol phosphate shuttle

In the cytoplasm the electrons are transferred from NADH₂ to dihydroxyacetone phosphate forming glycerol-3-phosphate, which is easily able to cross the outer mitochondrial membrane. This subsequently donates the electrons to the FAD located on the inner membrane, as shown by Figure 6.4.

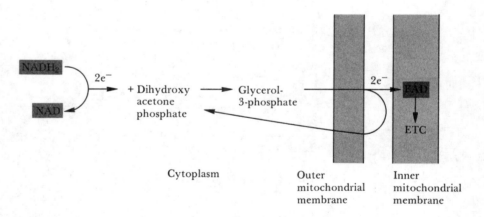

Figure 6.4   *The glycerol phosphate shuttle*

As you will recall FAD enters the ETC at a point after the first proton pump, and as a consequence only two ATPs are generated from the two cytoplasmic NADH₂ molecules if this shuttle is used. Under such circumstances the oxidation of one glucose molecule will only yield 36 molecules of ATP.

The malate shuttle

(The name 'malate shuttle' is commonly used, and to avoid confusion the '-ate' forms of malic acid, etc. are used in this section.) In the cytoplasm electrons from $NADH_2$ are transferred to oxaloacetate forming malate. This is able to cross the mitochondrial membranes and enter the matrix where it is reoxidised by mitochondrial NAD back to oxaloacetate, as shown by Figure 6.5. The $NADH_2$ formed by this reaction can now enter the ETC to produce three ATP molecules. The oxaloacetate must be converted to aspartate before it can be returned across the membrane to the cytoplasm. This is essential to maintain cytoplasmic stores of oxaloacetate. Consequently this may be referred to as the **malate–aspartate shuttle**.

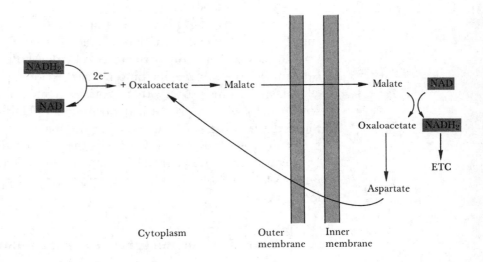

Figure 6.5   *The malate shuttle*

Since this series of reactions transfers the electrons to $NADH_2$ inside the mitochondrion, three ATP molecules are produced if this shuttle is used.

Why employ the glycerol phosphate shuttle when it costs an ATP molecule each time it's used?

Although the malate shuttle is cheaper to use in terms of ATP, it will only operate when the concentration of $NADH_2$ in the cytoplasm is higher than that in the mitochondrial matrix. This situation arises when the cell is actively respiring and consuming its mitochondrial

$NADH_2$ rapidly. This results in a much lower concentration of $NADH_2$ within the matrix and a higher concentration of free NAD (able to accept the electrons from malate), permitting the malate shuttle to operate. The net result is the maximum conservation of energy when energy demands are high.

If the mitochondrial membranes are impermeable, how do the ATP molecules synthesised inside the mitochondrion get to the cytoplasm where they are needed?

The exit of ATP from the mitochondrion is directly coupled to the entry of ADP from the cytoplasm via a special transport protein called ATP–ADP translocase.

The synthesis of ATP by the stalked particles requires a constant supply of ADP and inorganic phosphate (P_i). The ATP–ADP translocase binds readily with either ATP or ADP, depending on which side of the membrane its binding site is facing. If it is facing the cytoplasm it binds ADP, then 'rotates' (by conformational changes within the globular protein), depositing the ADP on the matrix side. Since the binding site is now facing the matrix it binds with an ATP molecule, rotates again, and deposits the ATP on the cytoplasmic side. In this way the mitochondrion is kept supplied with the raw materials it needs for ATP synthesis and the cytoplasm is supplied with the newly formed ATP.

How does the phosphate enter the mitochondrion?

The ATP–ADP translocase, together with the shuttles previously mentioned, represent only a fraction of the numerous carriers found within the mitochondrial membranes. Such carriers mediate the transfer of a variety of ions and molecules into and out of the mitochondrion. Glycerol-3-phosphate, pyruvic acid, malic acid, succinic acid, fumaric acid and citric acid as well as orthophosphate all traverse the mitochondrial membranes via carrier proteins.

Revision points

1   The flow of electrons through the ETC establishes a high concentration of protons in the fluid-filled intermembrane space of the mitochondrion.

2   The proton gradient has both electrical and chemical components. It is therefore called an **electrochemical gradient**.

3   Mitchell's **chemiosmotic theory** proposes that the inward flow of protons into the mitochondrial matrix is the mechanism linking electron flow to phosphorylation (ATP production).

4   The matrix side of the inner mitochondrial membrane is studded with numerous stalked particles (F_1—F_0 complexes). The F_0 stalk contains a proton channel and the F_1 head forms the enzyme ATP synthase.

5   Protons flow across the membrane via the proton channels running through these stalked particles.

6   The exact role of the protons is unclear but it now seems likely that they release the newly formed ATP which is tightly bound to ATP synthase heads.

7   The total ATP yield for the complete oxidation of one molecule of glucose is 38 ATP molecules.

8   The total ATP yield is reduced to 36, however, if cytoplasmic $NADH_2$ from glycolysis enters the mitochondrion via the glycerol phosphate shuttle.

9   The mitochondrial membranes contain a large number of globular transport proteins responsible for the transfer of metabolic intermediates, including ATP, into and out of the mitochondrion.

7 *Anaerobic respiration*

Anaerobic respiration

The role of oxygen in respiration is to serve as the final acceptor for hydrogen. Without oxygen, hydrogen atoms cannot be removed from the end of the ETC and it grinds to a halt (see chapter 5). With the ETC out of action reduced coenzyme ($NADH_2$/$FADH_2$) cannot be reoxidised and so eventually all the cell's reserves of coenzyme (NAD/FAD) will be in the reduced state. Without coenzyme to accept hydrogen atoms the reactions of the Krebs cycle cannot continue.

The net result is an accumulation of pyruvic acid, the end product of glycolysis.

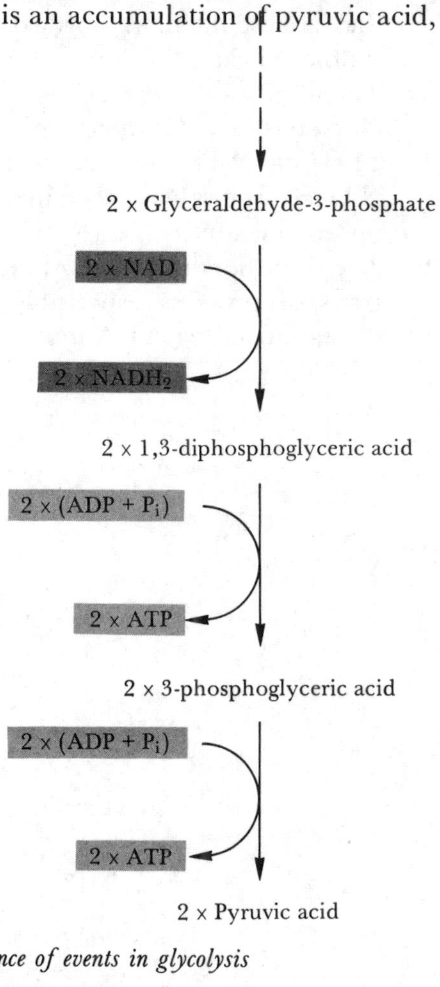

2 x Glyceraldehyde-3-phosphate

2 x NAD

2 x NADH$_2$

2 x 1,3-diphosphoglyceric acid

2 x (ADP + P$_i$)

2 x ATP

2 x 3-phosphoglyceric acid

2 x (ADP + P$_i$)

2 x ATP

2 x Pyruvic acid

Figure 7.1 *Sequence of events in glycolysis*

> # If there is no NAD available how can glycolysis continue to produce pyruvic acid?

As you can see from Figure 7.1 the two ATP-generating reactions of glycolysis occur after the dehydrogenation of the two molecules of glyceraldehyde-3-phosphate. Without NAD for this step glycolysis cannot proceed and no ATP will be made. Consequently an alternative means of reoxidising the $NADH_2$ must be found.

Pyruvic acid which has accumulated now serves as an alternative acceptor, reoxidising the $NADH_2$ to NAD. In this way a small quantity of NAD is made available allowing glycolysis to proceed even in the absence of oxygen, providing its small but possibly vital supply of ATP:

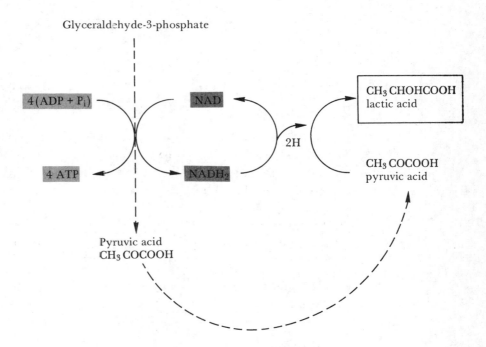

In animals the reduction of pyruvic acid leads to the formation of **lactic acid**. In plants, however, a different metabolic pathway operates converting the pyruvic acid to **ethanol** and **carbon dioxide**, a process termed **alcoholic fermentation**:

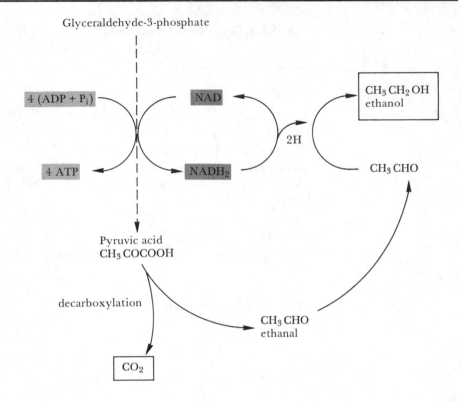

Since glycolysis is the only phase of respiration taking place anaerobic respiration only yields two molecules of ATP per glucose molecule. (*Remember*: Although four ATPs have been made, two are consumed in the initial phosphorylation reactions.)

What happens to the end products of anaerobic respiration?

In order to answer this we need to consider the fate of the end products in plants and animals separately.

Animals

Since only two ATPs have so far been released much of the potential energy yield of glucose remains trapped within lactic acid. This molecule represents a metabolic dead end and must be converted back to pyruvic acid before it can be metabolised and the energy it contains released. In addition its build-up in skeletal muscle lowers the pH, reducing the ability of the muscle fibres to contract and causing the aching sensation associated with fatigue.

Lactic acid rapidly accumulating in anaerobically respiring cells will readily diffuse through the plasma membrane into the bloodstream. On reaching the liver it is reoxidised to pyruvic acid by NAD, which is still available in the liver due to its lower metabolic demand (compared to actively contracting muscle). This pyruvic acid is then converted back to glucose by a series of reactions called **gluconeogenesis** (glucos = sugar, neo = new, genesis = creation, i.e. the creation of new sugar).

This process is essentially glycolysis in reverse, although by a slightly different pathway using different enzymes. The newly formed glucose is released into the bloodstream and returns to the muscles. This ensures that the level of glucose in the blood is maintained at a level sufficient to supply the needs of the anaerobically respiring muscle cells. This sequence of events is known as the **Cori cycle**, and is shown in Figure 7.2.

With the Cori cycle operating, why is it not possible for animals to maintain anaerobic respiration indefinitely?

The energy yield in anaerobic respiration is extremely small and is only a fraction of that normally provided by aerobic respiration. This means that the energy available to the tissue during anaerobiosis is insufficient to maintain all the metabolic processes essential to cell function. As a result cellular metabolism begins to run down, eventually leading to cell death. The fatiguing effect of large quantities of lactic acid therefore provides a vital early warning signal.

Once sufficient quantities of oxygen are made available the excess lactic acid produced by anaerobic respiration is converted to pyruvic acid. Some of this is then funnelled into the Krebs cycle to be fully oxidised to carbon dioxide and water, releasing a large quantity of ATP. This ATP provides the energy necessary to convert the remaining lactic acid to glucose via gluconeogenesis (an energy-expensive process). Any excess glucose formed in this way is converted to glycogen for storage in the liver and muscles.

During the anaerobic conversion of pyruvic acid to lactic acid the body is said to be incurring an **oxygen debt** (since pyruvic acid is now acting as the final hydrogen acceptor instead of oxygen). The reconversion of this lactic acid to pyruvic acid and then glucose requires oxygen, and the time taken for this conversion represents the time it takes for the body to repay its oxygen debt.

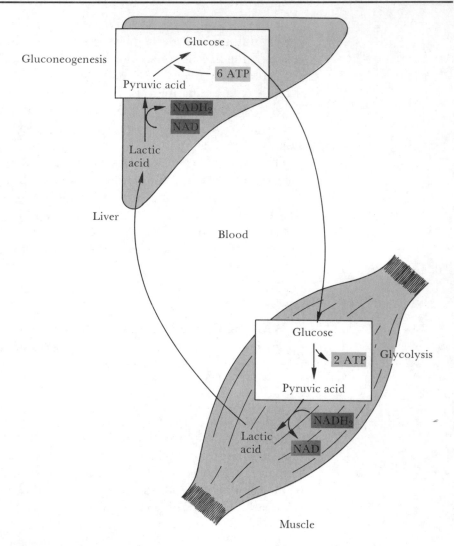

Figure 7.2   *The Cori cycle*

Plants

Unlike lactic acid, none of the energy trapped in ethanol is available to plants and since it is toxic it must be excreted along with the carbon dioxide produced. Alcoholic fermentation is commercially exploited in the brewing industry. Although microorganisms such as yeasts usually respire aerobically they can be made to respire anaerobically by placing them in airtight containers. Provided there is sufficient sugar available and the concentration of ethanol accumulating in the coning in the container is maintained below a critical level (approximately 12%), the yeast will continue to produce ethanol. Indeed the brewing industry devotes much time and effort to the development of yeasts with increased alcohol tolerance.

Summary of anaerobic respiration

Animals

$$CH_3COCOOH + NADH_2 \longrightarrow CH_3CHOHCOOH + NAD$$

pyruvic acid

lactic acid
(2-hydroxypropanoic acid)

product per glucose molecule: 2 lactic acid molecules

Plants

$$CH_3COCOOH \longrightarrow CH_3CHO + CO_2$$

pyruvic acid

$$\downarrow$$

$$CH_3CHO + NADH_2$$

ethanal

$$\downarrow$$

$$CH_3CH_2OH + NAD$$

ethanol

products per glucose molecule: 2 carbon dioxide molecules
2 ethanol molecules

Revision points

1   Anaerobic respiration occurs when there is insufficient oxygen for aerobic respiration to take place. Of the three main respiratory stages, only the glycolytic pathway operates.

2   Without oxygen to act as the final hydrogen acceptor the $NADH_2$ produced in glycolysis is reoxidised by pyruvic acid. This allows glycolysis to continue.

3   When pyruvic acid instead of oxygen accepts the hydrogen atoms from $NADH_2$, the body is said to be incurring an **oxygen debt**.

4   In animals the pyruvic acid is reduced to **lactic acid**.

5   In plants the pyruvic acid is reduced to **ethanol** and **carbon dioxide** is liberated – a process termed **alcoholic fermentation**.

6   In animals, during strenuous exercise the toxic lactic acid is recycled to glucose by **gluconeogenesis** in the liver and returned to the muscles via the bloodstream. This helps to maintain a supply of glucose to the actively respiring muscle. This sequence of events is called the **Cori cycle**.

7   Once sufficient oxygen is available the lactic acid which has accumulated in the muscles is converted back to pyruvic acid in the liver.

8   Some of this pyruvic acid is oxidised to carbon dioxide and water releasing sufficient energy to convert the remainder to glucose via gluconeogenesis.

9   Additional oxygen will continue to be taken in after exercise until all the lactic acid has been removed. In effect the body repays its oxygen debt.

10 Plants are unable to extract the energy trapped in ethanol and to prevent it accumulating to toxic levels it is excreted.

11 Compared with aerobic respiration, anaerobiosis is an inefficient process yielding only two ATPs per glucose molecule.

8 Alternative respiratory pathways

In the preceding chapters we have assumed that glucose alone serves as the respiratory substrate. In the living cell a much wider choice of fuels is available, ranging from the long hydrocarbon chains of fatty acids through simple sugars to the deaminated residues of amino acids. Each fuel is modified by a series of biochemical reactions until it is able to enter one of the familiar respiratory pathways. The biochemistry of many of these reactions is complex so we have endeavoured to provide no more than a brief summary of each of five major pathways:

(a)   Gluconeogenesis
(b)   Alternative sugar pathways
(c)   Lipid pathways
(d)   Protein pathways
(e)   Pentose phosphate pathway.

(a) Gluconeogenesis

This first pathway, shown in Figure 8.1, is not really an alternative but instead represents a means of converting certain non-carbohydrate compounds into glucose, which can then enter glycolysis.

Gluconeogenesis is not a direct reversal of glycolysis in that a new intermediate, **oxaloacetic acid**, is involved and several of the enzymes that catalyse the interconversions are different. In addition this pathway results in a net loss of six ATPs because the equilibrium of the glycolytic pathway lies far on the side of pyruvic acid formation. In other words pyruvic acid formation is favoured, so these reverse reactions are moving 'uphill' in energy terms. This process occurs primarily in the liver and kidney and serves to 'top up' blood glucose levels during anaerobic respiration (see chapter 7), and on those occasions when glycogen reserves are low. The body's reserves of the storage carbohydrate **glycogen** are normally sufficient for about a day. Periods of starvation longer than this will therefore rely heavily on gluconeogenesis for the maintenance of a constant blood sugar level.

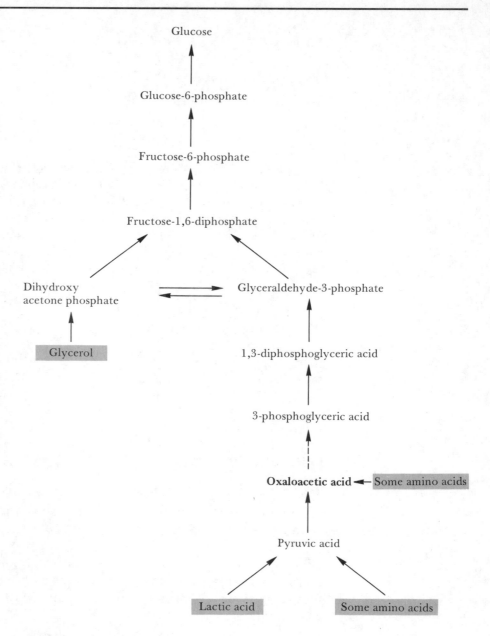

Figure 8.1   *Gluconeogenesis*

(b) *Alternative sugar pathways*

Many carbohydrate foodstuffs are rich not only in glucose but also in a variety of other sugars. The disaccharide **sucrose** (table sugar) consists of the monosaccharides fructose and glucose, and **lactose** (milk sugar) of galactose and glucose. Both galactose and fructose enter glycolysis, but by different routes.

Fructose-1-phosphate pathway

This pathway, shown in Figure 8.2, involves the splitting of phosphory-lated fructose into dihydroxyacetone phosphate and glyceraldehyde-3-phosphate and occurs primarily in the liver.

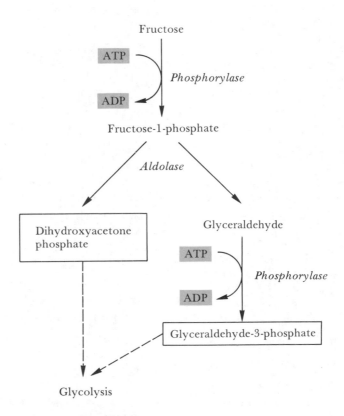

Figure 8.2   *The fructose-1-phosphate pathway*

Galactose–glucose interconversion pathway

Galactose is converted into glucose-1-phosphate in a series of complex reactions before being structurally rearranged (chapter 3, reaction 2) by an isomerase enzyme to form glucose-6-phosphate which is then able to enter glycolysis.

(c) Lipid pathways

Fat may be used as a respiratory fuel directly without first being converted to glucose. It is first hydrolysed by lipase enzymes into **fatty acids** and **glycerol**.

Lipid (triglyceride)   Glycerol   3 fatty acid molecules

The R groups represent long hydrocarbon chains of between 14 and 24 carbon atoms in length. They may even be identical, as in the case of the triglyceride triolein which consists of glycerol joined to three molecules of oleic acid.

Glycerol

Glycerol is converted into glyceraldehyde-3-phosphate, as shown in Figure 8.3, which is channelled into the glycolytic pathway (see chapter 3).

The ATP yield for the complete oxidation of glyceraldehyde-3-phosphate via glycolysis and the Krebs cycle is 17 ATPs. A further 3 ATPs will be generated from the reoxidation of the $NADH_2$ in the ETC, giving a total of 20 ATPs. One molecule of ATP was used in the initial phosphorylation of glycerol, resulting in a net yield of 19 ATPs per glycerol oxidised.

Fatty acids

The oxidation of fatty acids is a two-stage process involving a complex series of reactions. Firstly they are activated on the outer mitochondrial membrane by the attachment of coenzyme A to the carboxyl (COOH) end of the chain, as shown in Figure 8.4.

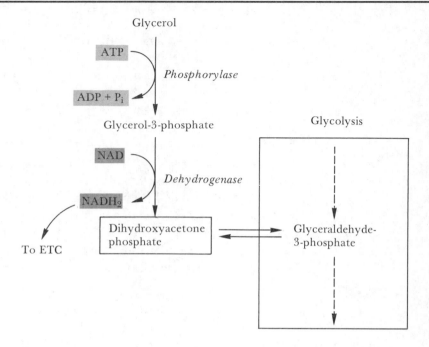

Figure 8.3   *The metabolism of glycerol*

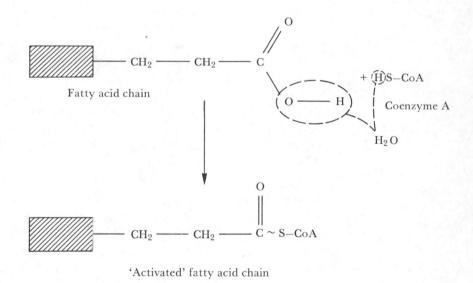

Figure 8.4   *Attachment of coenzyme A to a fatty acid*

These large molecules are then carried across the impermeable inner mitochondrial membrane by the carrier **carnitine** (a derivative of the amino acid lysine).

The second stage occurs inside the matrix and involves the shortening of the fatty acid chain by the removal of two carbon units at a time. The coenzyme A feeds the first two-carbon unit (as acetyl CoA) into the Krebs cycle by combining it with oxaloacetic acid (see chapter 4). This frees the coenzyme A to pick up the next two-carbon unit. In this way the fatty acid is oxidised by the repeated removal of two-carbon units which are converted into acetyl CoA and fed into the Krebs cycle – a process called **β-oxidation**. The energy yield for a single fatty acid molecule obviously depends on the length of the hydrocarbon chain and may well be over 140 ATPs. As a consequence fatty acids represent an extremely important source of energy, providing up to 50% of the energy requirement of some tissues.

(d)   *Protein pathways*

Unlike carbohydrates and fats, excess protein in the form of amino acids cannot be stored. Before amino acids can be metabolised the amino group (NH_2) must first be removed – a process called **deamination**. This produces highly toxic ammonia (NH_3) which is subsequently converted to less harmful **urea** in a complex series of reactions collectively called the **urea** or **ornithine cycle** (another Krebs discovery!). This is shown in Figure 8.5. The carbon skeleton of the amino acid is then converted to one of several respiratory intermediates, depending upon the number of carbon atoms it contains.

Those amino acids which liberate carbon skeletons made up of three carbon atoms may be converted into the respiratory intermediate pyruvic acid (3C). Those with four carbon atoms may be converted into oxaloacetic acid (4C), and the five-carbon amino acids into α-ketoglutaric acid (5C). The remaining carbon skeletons are converted into either acetyl CoA, succinyl CoA or fumaric acid for entry into the Krebs cycle.

Under conditions of severe starvation when carbohydrate and lipid stores are exhausted, tissue protein may undergo oxidation via these pathways in a final attempt to provide the energy necessary to maintain life processes.

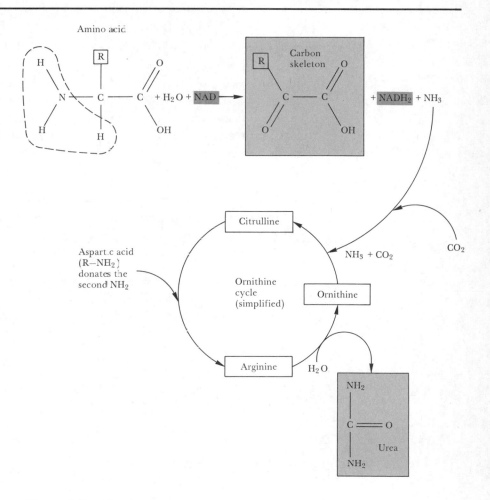

Figure 8.5 *Urea or ornithine cycle*

(e) *Pentose phosphate pathway (hexose monophosphate shunt)*

The **pentose phosphate pathway** is not just an alternative respiratory pathway since it also provides a mechanism by which glucose may be converted into other useful precursors, for example ribose-5-phosphate, a precursor of many important biomolecules including RNA, DNA, ATP, NAD, FAD and CoA. In other words, glucose is not just a fuel molecule but a potential source of many other useful biochemicals.

What determines whether glucose enters glycolysis or the pentose phosphate pathway?

The fate of the glucose depends upon the requirements of the cell. If energy demands are high the glucose will enter the normal glycolytic respiratory pathway and be completely oxidised to carbon dioxide and water. However, if the cell is actively synthesising large molecules it will require a supply of reducing power (hydrogen atoms). The pentose phosphate pathway generates this reducing power in the form of **nicotinamide adenine dinucleotide phosphate (NADPH$_2$)**. This is formed when glucose-6-phosphate is oxidatively decarboxylated (removal of hydrogen and carbon dioxide) to ribose-5-phosphate.

> **If the cell needs reducing power why doesn't it make use of the NADH$_2$ produced in glycolysis and the Krebs cycle?**

The advantage of producing the reducing power necessary for biosynthesis in this way is that ribose-5-phosphate can be recycled to form glucose-6-phosphate, or converted to glyceraldehyde-3-phosphate, as shown in Figure 8.6. This means reducing power has been obtained

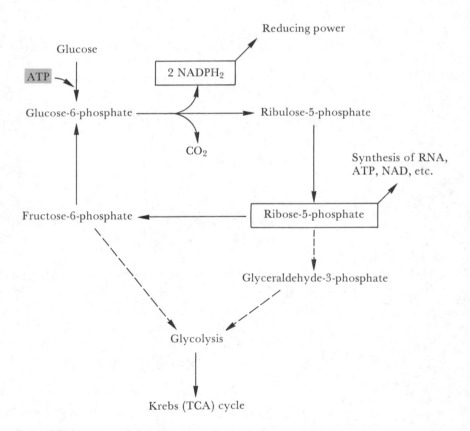

Figure 8.6 *Advantages of the pentose phosphate pathway*

without wasting any of the energy potential of the glucose molecules, since the recycled glucose-6-phosphate and any glyceraldehyde-3-phosphate can now enter the glycolytic pathway.

The pentose phosphate pathway is utilised much more frequently in tissues actively synthesising large molecules. For example, in adipose tissue the synthesis of long-chain fatty acids and steroids requires large quantities of hydrogen atoms which are supplied by $NADPH_2$.

Conversely, tissues with a high energy demand such as skeletal muscle have relatively low pentose phosphate activity, since the majority of available glucose is required for ATP production.

Summary of alternative respiratory pathways

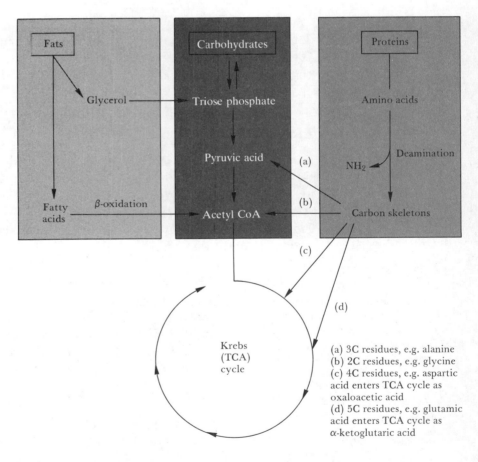

Figure 8.7   *Respiratory pathways for carbohydrate, fat and protein (simplified)*

Revision points

Gluconeogenesis

1 Gluconeogenesis provides a means of converting non-carbohydrate compounds into glucose.
2 Although it basically appears to be the glycolytic pathway in reverse, several different enzymes and a new intermediate (oxaloacetic acid) are involved.
3 The reverse pathway proceeds 'uphill' in energy terms and costs six ATPs.
4 It serves to 'top up' blood glucose levels during anaerobic respiration and periods of starvation.

Alternative sugar pathways

1 **Fructose** is phosphorylated and then split into dihydroxyacetone phosphate and glyceraldehyde-3-phosphate – both intermediates of glycolysis.
2 The fructose-1-phosphate costs two ATP molecules per fructose.
3 **Galactose** is converted to glucose-6-phosphate in a series of complex reactions. The glucose-6-phosphate is then able to enter glycolysis.

Lipid pathways

1 Triglycerides are first hydrolysed into fatty acids and glycerol.
2 **Glycerol** is converted into glyceraldehyde-3-phosphate which is a glycolytic intermediate.
3 A single glycerol molecule yields 19 ATPs.
4 **Fatty acids** must first be activated by the attachment of CoA to the carboxyl end of the chain.
5 In the mitochondrial matrix the fatty acid chain is broken down two carbon units at a time.
6 Each two-carbon unit is fed into the Krebs cycle by CoA to be completely oxidised in the usual way.
7 This process is called **β-oxidation** and may yield large numbers of ATP molecules depending upon the length of the fatty acid chain.

Protein pathways

1 Excess amino acids have their amino group (NH_2) removed by deamination leaving a carbon skeleton which can be fed into respiratory metabolism.

2   The carbon skeleton is converted into different respiratory intermediates depending upon the number of carbon atoms it contains.

3   The amino groups removed by deamination enter the ornithine cycle as ammonia (NH_3) where they are converted to urea for subsequent excretion.

Pentose phosphate pathway

1   Although not strictly a respiratory pathway, this provides a means of converting glucose to ribose-5-phosphate.

2   Ribose-5-phosphate is an important precursor molecule which can be used to build DNA, RNA, NAD, FAD, ATP and CoA at the expense of glucose molecules.

3   This conversion also produces reducing power in the form of reduced NADP ($NADPH_2$) – necessary for biosynthesis.

4   The advantage of generating reducing power ($NADPH_2$) in this way is that glucose may be resynthesised from those molecules of ribose-5-phosphate not used for biosynthesis. The potential energy yield of glucose is still available.

5   This pathway operates mostly in tissues that are actively synthesising large molecules. However, if energy demands are high glucose will tend to be channelled into the glycolytic pathway.

Appendix 1
Organic nomenclature

Organic compounds are named according to the number of carbon atoms they contain, for example:

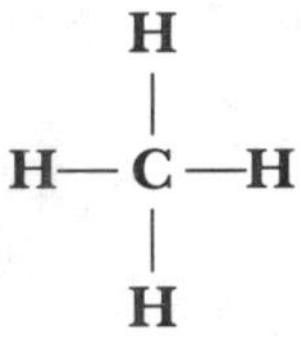

$$
\begin{array}{c}
H \\
| \\
H-C-H \\
| \\
H
\end{array}
$$

Methane CH_4

Note: The hydrogen atoms have been omitted from this point onwards and are represented by their bonds.

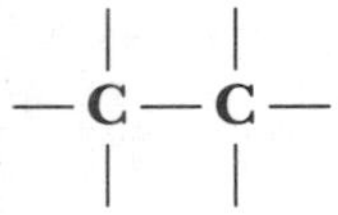

$$-C-C-$$

Ethane C_2H_6

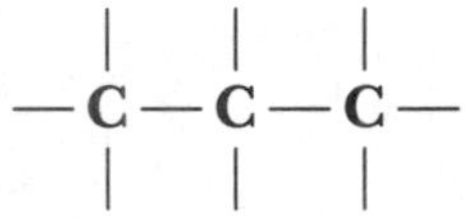

$$-C-C-C-$$

Propane C_3H_8

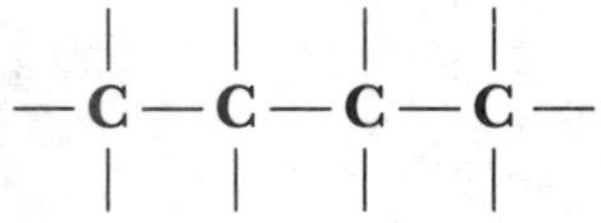

$$-C-C-C-C-$$

Butane C_4H_{10}

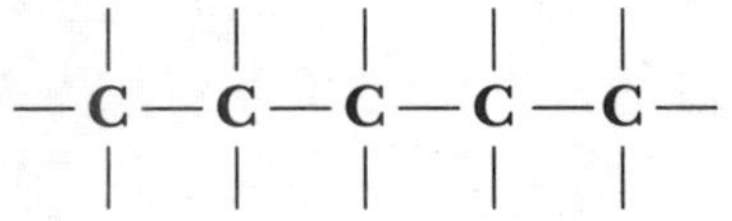

$$-C-C-C-C-C-$$

Pentane C_5H_{12}

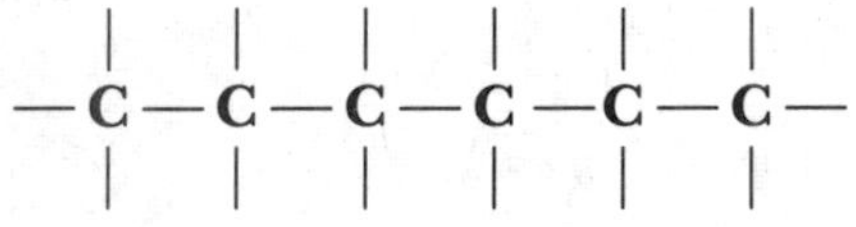

$$-C-C-C-C-C-C-$$

Hexane C_6H_{14}

$$-C-C-C-C-C-C-C-$$

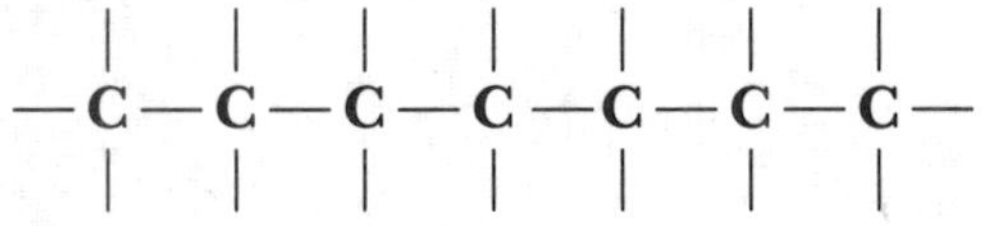

Heptane C_7H_{16}

$$-\overset{|}{\underset{|}{C}}-\overset{|}{\underset{|}{C}}-\overset{|}{\underset{|}{C}}-\overset{|}{\underset{|}{C}}-\overset{|}{\underset{|}{C}}-\overset{|}{\underset{|}{C}}-\overset{|}{\underset{|}{C}}-\overset{|}{\underset{|}{C}}-$$

Octane C_8H_{18}

$$-\overset{|}{\underset{|}{C}}-\overset{|}{\underset{|}{C}}-\overset{|}{\underset{|}{C}}-\overset{|}{\underset{|}{C}}-\overset{|}{\underset{|}{C}}-\overset{|}{\underset{|}{C}}-\overset{|}{\underset{|}{C}}-\overset{|}{\underset{|}{C}}-\overset{|}{\underset{|}{C}}-$$

Nonane C_9H_{20}

$$-\overset{|}{\underset{|}{C}}-\overset{|}{\underset{|}{C}}-\overset{|}{\underset{|}{C}}-\overset{|}{\underset{|}{C}}-\overset{|}{\underset{|}{C}}-\overset{|}{\underset{|}{C}}-\overset{|}{\underset{|}{C}}-\overset{|}{\underset{|}{C}}-\overset{|}{\underset{|}{C}}-\overset{|}{\underset{|}{C}}-$$

Decane $C_{10}H_{22}$

The first part of each name refers to the number of carbon atoms, while the second part refers to the bonding, for example:

$$-\overset{|}{\underset{|}{C}}-\overset{|}{\underset{|}{C}}-$$ **Ethane (single bond)**

$$\underset{/}{\overset{\backslash}{C}}=\underset{\backslash}{\overset{/}{C}}$$ **Ethene (double bond)**

$$-C\equiv C-$$ **Ethyne (triple bond)**

The names of organic compounds are modified according to any side groups attached. These also have their own terminology, as shown in Table A1.1.

Table A1.1   *Organic suffixes and prefixes*

Formula	Suffix	Prefix
—OOH	-oic acid	
—OO⁻	-oate (ion)	
—CHO	-al	oxo-
—CO	-one	oxo-
—OH	-ol	hydroxy-
—SH	-thiol	
—NH₂	-amine	amino-

Some common examples used in this book are given below.

Example 1

Ethanol CH_3CH_2OH

- starts with eth- (two carbons)
- single bonds (-an-)
- ends with -ol (alcohol group)

  i.e. eth-an-ol

Example 2

Ethanal CH_3CHO

- starts with eth- (two carbons)
- single bonds (-an-)
- ends with -al (aldehyde group)
  i.e. eth-an-al

Example 3

Lactic acid $CH_3CHOHCOOH$
(2-hydroxypropanoic acid)

- starts with prop- (three carbons)
- single bonds (-an-)
- ends with -oic acid (OOH)
  i.e. prop-an-oic acid

- but there is an alcohol group on the second carbon atom so it has the prefix 2-hydroxy-
  i.e. 2-hydroxy-prop-an-oic acid

Example 4

Pyruvic acid CH$_3$COCOOH
(2-oxopropanoic acid)

- starts with prop- (three carbons)
- single bonds (-an-)
- ends with -oic acid (OOH)
  i.e. prop-an-oic acid

- but there is a ketone group (CO) on the second carbon atom so it has the prefix 2-oxo
  i.e. 2-oxo-prop-an-oic acid

Example 5

Glycerol CH$_2$OH
       |
     CHOH
       |
     CH$_2$OH
(Propane-1, 2, 3-triol)

- starts with prop- (three carbons)

- single bonds (-an-)

- ends with -ol (OH)

  i.e. prop-an-ol

- but it has three alcohol groups (OH) instead of just one

This is written:

prop-ane-1,2,3-triol

Note: The carbon chain is numbered from whichever end gives the lowest prefix number.

Appendix 2
Enzyme classification

Table A2.1 *Enzyme classification*

Group	Reaction catalysed	Typical reaction	Enzyme example with trivial name
Oxidoreductase	Transfer of H and O atoms or electrons from one substance to another	$AH + B \rightleftharpoons A + BH$ reduced $A + O \rightleftharpoons AO$ oxidised	Dehydrogenase, oxidase
Transferase	Transfer of a specific group from one substance to another. The group may be methyl-, acyl-, amino- or phosphate	$AB + C \rightleftharpoons A + BC$	Transaminase, kinase
Hydrolase	Formation of two products from a substrate by hydrolysis	$AB + H_2O \rightleftharpoons AOH + BH$	Lipase, amylase, peptidase
Lyase	Non-hydrolytic addition or removal of groups from substrates. C—C, C—N, C—O or C—S bonds may be split	$$R-\overset{\overset{\textstyle O}{\|}}{C}-\underset{\underset{\textstyle OH}{\diagdown}}{C} \rightleftharpoons R-\underset{\underset{\textstyle H}{\diagdown}}{\overset{\overset{\textstyle O}{/\!/}}{C}} + CO_2$$	Decarboxylase, fumarase, aldolase
Isomerase	Intramolecular rearrangement	$AB \rightleftharpoons BA$	Isomerase, mutase
Ligase	Join together two molecules by synthesis of new C—O, C—S, C—N or C—C bonds with simultaneous breakdown of ATP	$X + Y + ATP \rightleftharpoons XY + ADP + P_i$	Synthetase

Appendix 3
Biochemical abbreviations

ADP	adenosine diphosphate
AMP	adenosine monophosphate
ATP	adenosine triphosphate
ATPase	adenosine triphosphatase
CoA	coenzyme A
Cyt	cytochrome
DNA	deoxyribonucleic acid
ETC	electron transfer chain
FAD	flavin adenine dinucleotide (oxidised)
FADH$_2$	flavin adenine dinucleotide (reduced)
FMN	flavin mononucleotide (oxidised)
FMNH$_2$	flavin mononucleotide (reduced)
NAD	nicotinamide adenine dinucleotide (oxidised)
NADH$_2$	nicotinamide adenine dinucleotide (reduced)
NADP	nicotinamide adenine dinucleotide phosphate (oxidised)
NADPH$_2$	nicotinamide adenine dinucleotide phosphate (reduced)
P$_i$	inorganic orthophosphate (HPO_4^{2-})
Q	ubiquinone (coenzyme Q)
RNA	ribonucleic acid
RQ	respiratory quotient
TCA	tricarboxylic acid (cycle)

Appendix 4
Respiratory quotient

The **respiratory quotient** is the ratio of carbon dioxide produced by metabolism to oxygen consumed over a set time period:

$$RQ = \frac{\textbf{volume/moles CO}_2 \textbf{ produced}}{\textbf{volume/moles O}_2 \textbf{ consumed}}$$

RQ values give an indication of the nature of the respiratory substrate and the type of metabolism involved. Theoretical RQ values for the complete oxidation of pure carbohydrate, protein and fat can be calculated from the relevant chemical equations. For example, for the complete oxidation of glucose:

$$C_6H_{12}O_6 + 6O_2 \longrightarrow 6CO_2 + 6H_2O$$

$$RQ = \frac{\textbf{mol CO}_2 \textbf{ produced}}{\textbf{mol O}_2 \textbf{ consumed}} = \frac{6CO_2}{6O_2} = 1$$

The RQ for the complete oxidation of glucose (and also other carbohydrates) is 1.

Similarly the complete oxidation of the fatty acid palmitic acid can be calculated:

$$C_{16}H_{32}O_2 + 23O_2 \longrightarrow 16CO_2 + 16H_2O$$

palmitic acid

$$RQ = \frac{16CO_2}{23O_2} = 0.70$$

The RQ for the complete oxidation of palmitic acid (and also other fats) is 0.7.

Calculation of the RQ value for proteins is complicated by the fact that proteins are not completely oxidised since part of the molecule (the amino group, removed at deamination) is excreted from the body as nitrogenous waste. The amount of ingested protein and the quantity of nitrogenous waste excreted need to be known before the RQ value can be calculated.

Typical values for the oxidation of protein are approximately 0.8.

Table A4.1   *Respiratory quotients*

Substrate	RQ
Carbohydrate	1.0
Fat	0.7
Protein	0.8

In practice, values of between 0.8 and 0.9 are obtained from living organisms. This suggests that at any one time a mixture of substrates is being oxidised, primarily carbohydrates and fats.

RQ values greater than 1.0 indicate that more carbon dioxide is being produced than oxygen consumed. This situation arises during anaerobic respiration or when organisms are building up a store of food reserves, since the conversion of carbohydrate to fat liberates carbon dioxide.

Appendix 5 Glycolysis and the Krebs cycle (in full)

Figure A5.1 shows glycolysis and the Krebs cycle in full. Table A5.1 gives the trivial and systematic names of the principal intermediates and Table A5.2 the names of the principal enzymes.

Table A5.1 *Nomenclature of main intermediates of glycolysis and the Krebs cycle*

Trivial names	Systematic names
Glycerol	Propane-1,2,3-triol
Pyruvic acid	2-oxopropanoic acid
Citric acid	2-hydroxypropane-1,2,3-tricarboxylic acid
Fumaric acid	Trans-butenedioic acid
Isocitric acid	1-hydroxypropane-1,2,3-tricarboxylic acid
α-ketoglutaric acid	1-oxobutanedioic acid
Malic acid	2-hydroxybutanedioic acid
Oxaloacetic acid	2-oxobutanedioic acid
Oxalosuccinic acid	1-oxopropane-1,2,3-tricarboxylic acid
Succinic acid	Butanedioic acid

Table A5.2 *Principal enzymes of glycolysis and the Krebs cycle*

1	Glyceraldehyde phosphate dehydrogenase + NAD
2	Phosphoglyceric phosphokinase
3	Phosphoglyceromutase
4	Enolase + Mg^{2+}
5	Pyruvic phosphokinase + K^+
6	Pyruvate dehydrogenase + NAD Pyruvate decarboxylase + TPP
7	Citrate synthase
8	Aconitase
9	Aconitase
10	Isocitrate dehydrogenase + NAD or NADP
11	Oxalosuccinate decarboxylase
12	α-ketoglutarate dehydrogenase + NAD α-ketoglutarate decarboxylase + TPP
13	Succinyl CoA synthetase
14	Succinate dehydrogenase + FAD
15	Fumarase
16	Malate dehydrogenase + NAD

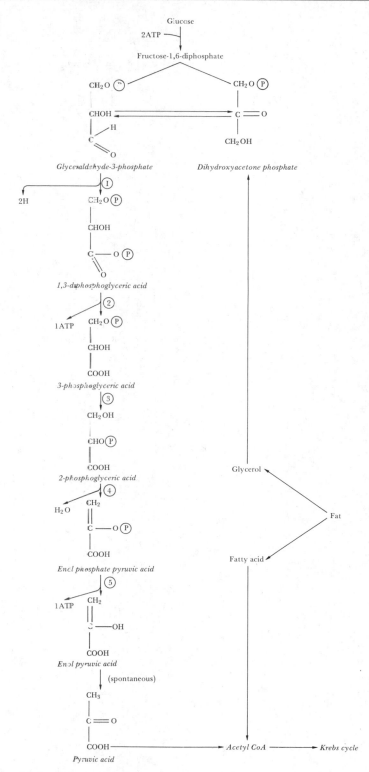

Figure A5.1   *Glycolysis and the Krebs cycle in full*

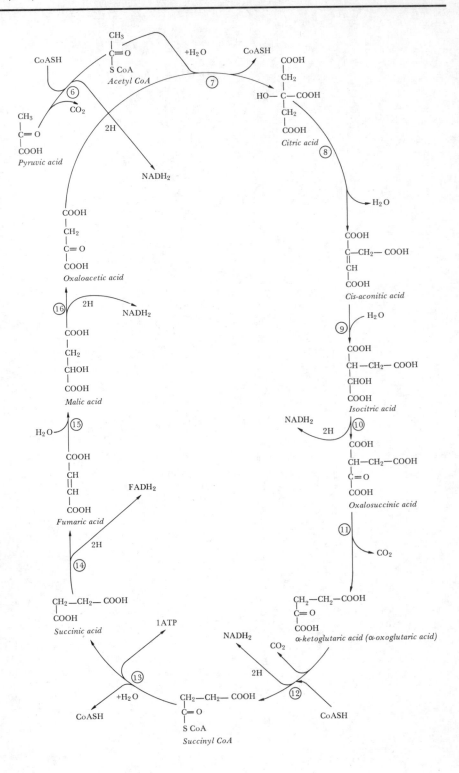

Appendix 6 Aerobic respiration (in summary)

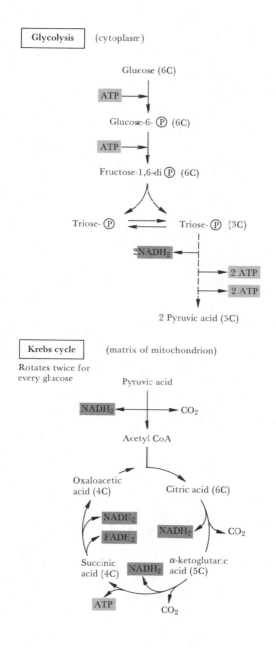

Products per glucose molecule	ATP yield
2 ATP	2
2NADH$_2$	6
2NADH$_2$ 2CO$_2$	6
2ATP 6NADH$_2$ 2FADH$_2$ 4CO$_2$	2 18 4
Total	38

Glycolysis   (cytoplasm)

Glucose (6C)

ATP

Glucose-6- P (6C)

ATP

Fructose-1,6-di P (6C)

Triose- P   Triose- P (3C)

2NADH$_2$

2 ATP

2 ATP

2 Pyruvic acid (3C)

Krebs cycle   (matrix of mitochondrion)

Rotates twice for every glucose

Pyruvic acid

NADH$_2$ → CO$_2$

Acetyl CoA

Oxaloacetic acid (4C)

Citric acid (6C)

NADH$_2$

FADH$_2$

NADH$_2$ → CO$_2$

Succinic acid (4C)

NADH$_2$

α-ketoglutaric acid (5C)

ATP

CO$_2$

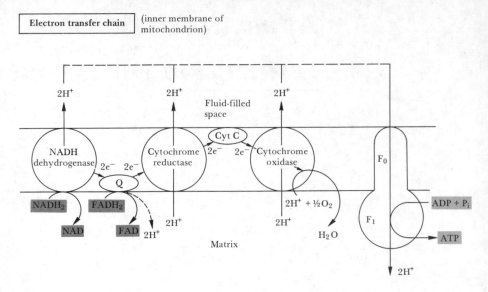

Figure A6.1 *Aerobic respiration in summary*

Appendix 7
Metabolic pathways

There are many complex metabolic pathways in the body, in which glycolysis and the Krebs cycle play a central role. An outline is given in Figure A7.1.

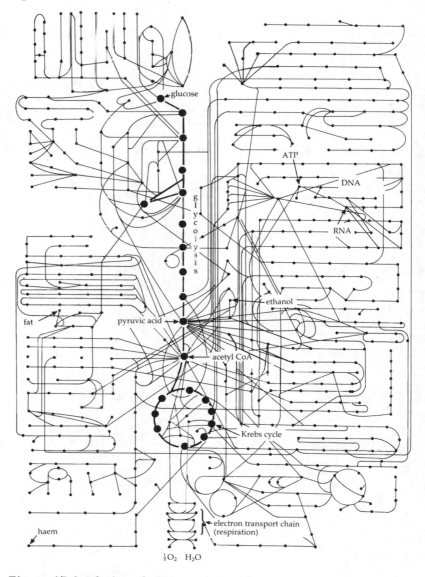

Figure A7.1   *Outline of major metabolic pathways*

Suggestions for further reading

Standard advanced level texts

'A' Level Biology   (1989) W. D. Phillips, T. J. Chilton.
                                        Oxford University Press.

Biological Science   (1990) N. P. O. Green, G. W. Stout, D. J. Taylor.
Volumes 1 and 2   Cambridge University Press.

Biology   (1983) 4th Edition, H. Curtis. Worth Publications.

Biology   (1983) 5th Edition, J. W. Kimball. Addison Wesley
                                        Publications.

Biology: A Functional Approach   (1986) 4th Edition, M. B. V. Roberts. Nelson.

Understanding Biology for Advanced   (1987) G. Toole, S. Toole. Stanley Thornes
Level   (Publishers) Ltd.

Specific reading

Biology of Respiration   (1980) 2nd Edition, A. Bryant. *Studies in Biology* series
                                        number 28. Edward Arnold.

Enzymes, Energy and Metabolism   (1986) M. R. Ingle. *Advanced Studies in Biology* series
                                        number 3. Basil Blackwell.

Guidebook to Biochemistry   (1980) 4th Edition, M. Yudkin, R. Offord. Cambridge
                                        University Press.

How Cells Make ATP   (1978) P. C. Hinkle, R. E. McCarty. *Scientific American*
                                        238. W. H. Freeman and Co.

Introducing Biochemistry   (1982) E. G. Wood, W. R. Pickering. John Murray
                                        Publications.

Degree level texts

Animal Physiology	(1983) 2nd Edition, R. Eckert, D. Randall. W. H. Freeman and Co.
Animal Physiology	(1983) 3rd Edition, K. Schmidt-Nielson. Cambridge University Press.
Principles of Biochemistry	(1982) 3rd Edition, A. L. Lehninger. Worth Publications.
Biochemistry	(1988) 3rd Edition, L. Stryer. W. H. Freeman and Co.
Cells and Organelles	(1976) 2nd Edition, A. B. Novikoff, E. Holtzman. Holt, Rinehart, Winston Publications.
Molecular Biology of the Cell	(1989) 2nd Edition, B. Alberts *et al*. Garland Publications.

Index